W9-ARL-216

GRADE 8 FCAT

READING AND WRITING+

Kelly Battles, B.A.
Former 8th Grade Language Arts Teacher
Fruit Cove Middle School
St. Johns County

BARRON'S

Copyright © 2006 by Barron's Educational Series, Inc.

All rights reserved. No part of this book may be reproduced in any form, by photostat, microfilm, xerography, or any other means, or incorporated into any information retrieval system, electronic or mechanical, without the written permission of the copyright owner.

All inquiries should be addressed to:
Barron's Educational Series, Inc.
250 Wireless Boulevard
Hauppauge, New York 11788
http://www.barronseduc.com

ISBN-13: 978-0-7641-3316-9
ISBN-10: 0-7641-3316-0

Library of Congress Catalog Card No. 2005053609

Library of Congress Cataloging-in-Publication Data

Battles, Kelly A., 1974-
    Grade 8 FCAT reading and writing+ / Kelly A. Battles.
      p. cm.
    At head of title: Barron's.
    ISBN 0-7641-3316-0
      1. Language arts (Middle school)—Florida—Examinations—Study guides. 2. Florida
        Comprehensive Assessment Test—Study guides. I. Title: Barron's Grade 8 FCAT reading and
        writing+. II. Title.

    LB1631.5.B38 2006
    373.126'2—dc22

                                                  2005053609

Printed in the United States of America

9 8 7 6 5 4 3 2 1

Contents

Chapter 1

Introduction

HOW TO USE THIS BOOK

 Before you begin reading and practicing for the different parts of the Florida Comprehensive Assessment Test (FCAT), turn to the back of the book and take Practice Test One. It's important that you time yourself while you take each practice test and that you do not go over the allowed time. Follow the directions for each section and record your answers in the answer booklet included.

After you have completed each section of Practice Test One, stop and score yourself using the answers provided and the self-scoring rubrics. When you're through, take time to read the explanations for the questions you missed. This time of "self-reflection" will help you identify the areas you should continue to practice. And by taking the time to learn why you missed an answer, you will increase your chance of scoring well on the FCAT.

When you are finished with the chapters and practice exercises, turn to the back of the book and take Practice Test Two. After completing each section of this test, stop and score yourself using the answers provided and the self-scoring rubrics. Take time to read the explanations for the questions you missed so that you know in what areas you must still work and practice.

Each of the steps in this process will help you to become a better reader and a more effective writer.

FREQUENTLY ASKED QUESTIONS

What Is the FCAT?

All portions of the FCAT SSS are based on the Florida Comprehensive Assessment Test Sunshine State Standards. These standards identify the specific academic skills you must develop in order to be successful on the FCAT. These are also skills that will help you succeed in life.

The FCAT is Florida's way of measuring your knowledge in an objective, uniform way as compared to that of students across the state. It also keeps the public schools accountable for teaching the appropriate skills you need to succeed in the future.

Each Florida public school is required to include all the Sunshine State Standards in its curriculum.

The Grade 8 FCAT is made up of five tests: Reading, Writing+ (Essay), Writing+ (Multiple Choice), Science, and Math. This book will provide instruction and practice in the following:

- **FCAT Reading:** a test that measures your knowledge of reading. This includes literary knowledge as well as informational knowledge. Literary works included on the test are fictional poems, short stories, folktales, and excerpts from novels. Informational texts consist of nonfictional magazine and newspaper articles, as well as biographies and editorials. The subject of all FCAT reading material covers the major content areas: science, mathematics, language arts, and social studies. The types of questions in this section include multiple choice, short response, and extended response.
- **FCAT Writing +:** two tests that measure your writing ability and your knowledge of writing conventions. The essay portion is a test that measures your ability to write an essay in response to a persuasive or expository prompt. The other Writing+ Test includes multiple-choice questions. This test assesses your knowledge of the rules of grammar, as well as your ability to put proper grammar into use.

Who Should Take the FCAT?

Every Florida public school student in a tested grade must take the FCAT (with few exceptions). Extra services are provided for those students who need them. Ask your teacher or guidance counselor for more information.

When and Where Is the FCAT Given?

In February and March of each year, the FCAT is administered in public schools across the state. In most schools, the homeroom teacher administers the test.

Why Are the Grade 8 FCAT Reading and Writing+ Tests Important?

The Grade 8 FCAT determines your reading and writing ability. The test is not to see how well you study for tests; it is truly used to measure what you already know. It also lets schools and teachers know if they are providing instruction that meets the state's standards.

The results of your test may be used in school for placement. Your school's grade is partially determined based on its students' FCAT scores.

It is important to note that taking these tests prepares you for the Grade 10 FCAT, which you must pass in order to graduate from high school.

What Is the FCAT Reading Test?

On the FCAT Reading Test, you will be given between six and eight reading passages of various lengths, averaging 700 words each. Sixty percent will be informational texts such as magazine and newspaper articles, editorials, and biographies. The remaining 40 percent of the passages will be literary texts, including short stories, poems, folktales, fables, or selections from novels.

You will be asked to answer between 45 and 50 multiple-choice questions. These questions make up 85 percent of the FCAT Reading Test. Each multiple-choice question will have four answer choices. Never leave any blank answers. You will not be penalized for guessing on this test. Go with your first thought on an answer and change it only if you are certain that you are wrong. Statistics show that your gut reaction is usually right.

Only 15 percent (anywhere from 5 to 8) of the questions are "performance tasks." These include extended-response and short-response items. Each performance task asks you to explain in your own words your answer to a question.

All these answers are explained in more detail in Chapter 2: Taking the FCAT Reading Test.

What Is FCAT Writing+?

FCAT Writing+ is the new name for the writing test of the FCAT. This test is made up of two parts: an essay and multiple-choice questions.

For the essay portion, you will be required to answer only one essay prompt that is broken up into a "Writing Situation" and "Directions for Writing." You will be given either an expository or a persuasive topic about which to write.

The multiple-choice questions will have either three or four choices. They will test your knowledge of writing skills directly, in a way that your written essay cannot.

All these answers are explained in more detail in Chapters 3 and 4.

When Will I Receive My FCAT Scores?

Usually before school is out for the year, you will receive your FCAT scores. Your teacher or guidance counselor will distribute scores to students in a timely manner.

What Is a Passing Score on the FCAT and Must I Pass the Grade 8 FCAT Tests?

You will receive a score between 100 and 500 on the FCAT Reading Test, with 500 being the highest score possible. This is your "scale score" based on the number of correct answers.

On the FCAT Writing+ Test (Essay), you will earn a score from 0 to 6, with 6 being the highest score possible.

Because there is no passing scale score for the Grade 8 FCAT test at this time, your score on the test will not determine whether or not you pass the eighth grade. However, in the tenth grade, you *will* be required to pass the FCAT. If you do not pass the Grade 10 FCAT, you will be given several chances before the end of twelfth grade to take the test until you do pass it. Otherwise, you will not graduate.

How Do I Interpret the Sunshine State Standards Benchmark Coding System?

The first two letters, "LA," stand for the subject area (Language Arts). The next letter represents the strand (Reading, Writing, or Literature), followed by the number of the standard, then the developmental level, and finally the actual benchmark number.

Note this example:

LA.A.1.3.2. The student uses background knowledge of the subject and text structure knowledge to make complex predictions of content, purpose, and organization.

LA: The subject area is Language Arts.
A: The strand is Reading.
1: This is the first standard in the Reading strand.
3: The level is 3 (which is the level for grades 6 through 8; this number always stays the same).
2: This is the second benchmark under this specific standard.

All the Grade 8 Sunshine State Standards for Language Arts are listed in the appendix.

How Should I Prepare for the FCAT?

In the next few chapters, you will learn specific strategies to put into practice on the test. These strategies will help you be better prepared for the actual test. Knowing what to expect also calms your nerves on test day!

The chapters on the specific FCAT tests will guide you through practices of all the different types of questions and prompts on the FCAT. This will give you many opportunities to "Try, try, again!" Remember, your mind is a muscle, and by "working it out," you are bound to get better.

Chapter 5 will help you understand how the FCAT is scored and how you can score your best on test day. Knowing how your essay will be scored gives you an advantage in trying to write the best essay possible. And knowing what the evaluator is looking for in your essay will make it easier to write on test day.

When you take each of the practice tests in the back of the book, take your time because you are practicing these questions for the first time. However, time yourself and make your surroundings as similar as you can to your classroom (or wherever you will take the test). This will give you the best indication of how you will actually do on test day. Your score will show you what improvements you've made and if you still have any weaknesses to work on. Be sure to read through the explanations of the answers for each question you missed. Use the self-scoring guide to score your essay and your performance task answers. You may also want to ask your parents to score your written answers; then take the average score.

If there are areas where you still need improvement, ask your teacher for help or visit www.fcatexplorer.com.

Chapter 2

Taking the FCAT Reading Test

When you take the FCAT, the Reading test will evaluate your ability to read different types of texts and your ability to answer different types of questions about these texts. This section of the FCAT is made up of 45 to 50 multiple-choice questions. This chapter will guide you through preparation in how to read passages and answer various types of questions—multiple choice, short response, and extended response. Each answer is worth between 1 and 4 points, so make sure you answer all the questions by bubbling in an answer choice or writing as much as you can on the lines provided.

You will be allowed two 80-minute sessions for this test. Be sure to read each text before answering the questions about it. In this chapter, you will learn important prereading techniques. There is even a bookmark with these guidelines in the appendix. After reading the texts, you should then go through the questions and choose the best answer. If you are unsure of an answer, take a guess, but mark it in your booklet so that you can come back to it at the end.

Throughout this chapter, you will learn how to prepare for the four major reading skills tested: words and phrases in context; main idea, plot, and purpose; comparison/contrast and cause/effect; and reference/research. Each skill will be explained, and examples will be presented. Then, you will focus in on the specific skills with guided practice. Take the time to read the information presented and to study each example before practicing. Finally, you will

> Tip: Multiple-choice answers are worth 1 point; short-response answers are worth up to 2 points; extended-response answers are worth up to 4 points.

be asked to read three different texts and answer questions about each one. Check all your answers against those on pages 35–37 to monitor your progress.

TYPES OF TEXTS

Tip: In the FCAT Reading Test the text is made up of 40 percent literary texts and 60 percent informational texts.

Literary texts include

- short stories
- poems
- selections from novels
- fables and folktales
- literary essays
- plays
- historical fiction

Informative texts include

- magazine articles
- newspaper articles
- biographies and autobiographies
- editorials
- primary sources
- tables and graphs
- "how to" articles
- ads
- consumer materials
- informational essays
- diaries
- subject area text

CHOOSING THE CORRECT ANSWER (MULTIPLE-CHOICE QUESTIONS)

- Do not to leave any stray marks around the answer bubbles. Fill them in neatly.

correct way to bubble-in an answer   incorrect bubbling-in with stray marks

- As you go through the questions, mark an answer for each and every question; if you are not positive of an answer, mark it in your booklet and be sure to come back to it later.
- Never leave any blanks. Always make a guess.
- When you are unsure of an answer, eliminate as many choices as you can before you make a guess.
- If there is time, go back and make sure that you have given the best possible answer for each question.
- Remember, there is only one correct answer for every question. Your job is to choose that answer!

STRATEGIES FOR READING

Prereading

One of the most important parts of reading is prereading. Prereading includes

- reading the title and all headings or subheadings in the passage.
- looking at all the pictures, captions, and graphics included with the passage.
- reading the whole passage once before you answer any of the questions.

Reading

Tip: A bookmark reminder can be found in the appendix.

There are many strategies for improving your reading comprehension. The following method will help you find important information to answer the questions. Practice the following activities and see if it improves your reading ability. You must decide if using the strategies will help you on test day or not.

- Underline main ideas once.
- Underline supporting details and examples twice.
- Circle any words that aren't familiar to you. These words may be used in questions designed to see if you can construct meaning from the text. If you can find a

word quickly in the story, it will be easier for you to determine its meaning. Use all the pictures and/or graphics included in the story as well.

- ▪ Box dates and/or numbers.
- ▪ Write a brief summary in the margin (one to two sentences to help you remember the main points of the story).

Example

266 Feet in the Air

From the Pittsburgh Commercial Gazette, *17 June 1893. Special to the Commercial Gazette.*

Chicago, June 16.—Standing on a chair in a car swaying 266 feet above the earth a little woman raised a glass of champagne to her lips and drank to the health of her husband. The little woman looked wonderfully pretty. Her eyes shone with the light of love and wifely pride. She smiled sweetly at those in the cars beneath her and they cheered wildly for her and her husband. She was dressed in a dainty gown of black, trimmed with gold. She said softly as she made the toast: "To the health of my husband and the success of the Ferris wheel."

She wasn't a bit afraid as she stood there, and that alone shows the immense amount of faith she must have in George W. S. [sic] Ferris, both as husband and mechanical engineer. Her black eyes sparkled deliciously as she made the toast and the bright color shown in her cheeks and the mist-laden wind played tenderly with her dark curls.

Reading Practice

Now it's your turn. Using the guidelines, circle, underline, and so on, all the specified information in the rest of the article about the Ferris wheel. You can check the answers later in the chapter for a sample of what could have been underlined, circled, and so on.

Some Were Timid

Then two-score invited guests filed in, their faces expressing all the emotions, ranging from pleased expectancy to a very palpable timidity. Then a second car was swung to the landing and more guests piled in. Some men with voices of marked huskiness shouted unintelligible orders to each other and the great wheel began to revolve for the first time.

It was 6:32 o'clock. Slowly, almost imperceptibly, it lifted the cars away from the earth, revolving from east to west. A fourth of the way up the wheel stopped. The passengers gasped in unison and looked at each other with smiles more or less sickly. They looked down and saw that they were hanging directly over the Austrian village. Suddenly they heard the regular throbbing of the engines again and felt much better.

The wheel climbed steadily upward and the passengers grew bolder. Some of them looked over the edge of the car and at once became less bold. In eight minutes the wheel had completed the first quarter of the circle. In seven minutes more the loaded cars had measured half the circumference and hung 266 feet above the earth.

Again the engines stopped and the champagne was poured. All in the two cars drank standing to George W. S. [sic] Ferris, Mrs. Ferris proposing the toast and calling it across to those in the next car. Then all gave three cheers to the inventor and drank to the health of his pretty wife with immense enthusiasm.

SKILLS TESTED ON THE FCAT READING TEST

On the FCAT Reading Test, four major skills are tested: words and phrases in context; main idea, plot, and purpose; comparison/contrast and cause/effect; and reference/research. This next section will take you through each skill individually and provide practice. Always check your answers so that you know where you need more help.

Words and Phrases in Context

You will be evaluated on how well you are able to

Tip: Fifteen to twenty percent of the questions will test your ability to use words and phrases in context.

- analyze vocabulary words from the text.
- analyze the text itself by using clues from the text.
- come to a conclusion about the text.

If you have made it a habit to circle words you don't know in a text, it should be a breeze to find them when they appear in a test question. In order to determine the meaning of one of these words, first look at the words surrounding it. Then look at pictures, charts, or graphs to help you determine the meaning. You will practice this skill later in this chapter.

Another way to prepare for FCAT Reading Test questions that ask you to analyze words is to enrich your vocabulary. There are many ways to do this, including

- *Studying vocabulary*: Whenever you find a word you do not know, write it down in a notebook and look up the definition. This will train you to stop and look up words you don't know.
- *Looking at the prefixes and suffixes of a word*: Many times, the meaning of a word has been changed by adding a prefix or suffix.
- *Making flashcards*: Write each vocabulary word on one side of an index card, and the definition on the other.
- *Using vocabulary words in everyday situations*: If you use a new word three times, you are more likely to add that word to your working vocabulary.

▪ *Studying the terms in the glossary of this book*:
Knowing the terms ("analyze," "persuasive," and so
on) used throughout the test will make you more comfortable when trying to answer the questions.

Vocabulary Practice

Read the following sentences and choose the correct
answer. Check your answers when you are finished. (The
sentences come from the article on the Ferris wheel that
you previously read in this chapter.)

1. What is the meaning of the word "dainty" in the sen-
   tence "She was dressed in a dainty gown of black,
   trimmed with gold"?
   A. small
   B. large
   C. expensive
   D. fancy

2. What is the meaning of the word "immense" in the
   sentence "She wasn't a bit afraid as she stood there,
   and that alone shows the immense amount of faith
   she must have in George W. S. [sic] Ferris, both as
   husband and mechanical engineer"?
   F. little
   G. great
   H. lack of
   I. undermining

3. What is the meaning of the word "gasped" in the
   sentence "The passengers gasped in unison and
   looked at each other with smiles more or less sickly"?
   A. whispered
   B. yelled
   C. blew out air with shock
   D. breathed in air with shock

4. What is the meaning of the word "unintelligble" in the sentence "Some men with voices of marked huskiness shouted unintelligible orders to each other and the great wheel began to revolve for the first time"?
F. demanding
G. able to be understood
H. not able to be understood
I. unreasonable

5. What is the meaning of the word "throbbing" in the sentence "Suddenly they heard the regular throbbing of the engines again and felt much better"?
A. dripping
B. beating
C. humming
D. singing

Main Idea, Plot, and Purpose

Tip: Thirty to fifty-five percent of the questions will test your understanding of the main idea, plot, and purpose of a text.

You will be evaluated on how well you are able to

■ determine the stated or implied main idea.
■ identify details and facts that are important to the main idea.
■ recognize organizational patterns.
■ recognize persuasive text.
■ recognize and understand how literary elements support text.
■ identify the author's purpose.
■ identify the point of view.

Let's break down the three basic skills discussed in this section (main idea, plot, and purpose):

MAIN IDEA

Understanding the main idea of a text is a very important skill. Sometimes the main idea is stated plainly, but other times it must be inferred. To find a main idea that must be inferred, look at the topic sentences of each paragraph or locate the overall topic sentence of the passage, often found in the introductory paragraph.

In order to increase your understanding of what you read,

- ▪ underline the main ideas once in a passage.
- ▪ summarize the story in one or two sentences.

PLOT

The plot of a passage includes the time, place, people, or events in the text. If you have underlined details twice while reading the passage, you should be able to locate this information quickly in response to the questions.

PURPOSE

The author had a specific purpose in mind when he or she wrote the text. These are the major types of purposes of writing:

- ▪ to inform
- ▪ to entertain
- ▪ to persuade
- ▪ to explain or describe

Main Idea/Plot/Purpose Practice

Reread the article on the Ferris wheel and answer the questions that follow. Check your answers against the answers provided.

266 Feet in the Air

From the Pittsburgh Commercial Gazette, *17 June 1893.
Special to the Commercial Gazette.*

Chicago, June 16.—Standing on a chair in a car swaying 266 feet above the earth a little woman raised a glass of champagne to her lips and drank to the health of her husband. The little woman looked wonderfully pretty. Her eyes shone with the light of love and wifely pride. She smiled sweetly at those in the cars beneath her and they cheered wildly for her and her husband. She was dressed in a dainty gown of black, trimmed with gold. She said softly as she made the toast: "To the health of my husband and the success of the Ferris wheel."

She wasn't a bit afraid as she stood there, and that alone shows the immense amount of faith she must have in George W. S. [sic] Ferris, both as husband and mechanical engineer. Her black eyes sparkled deliciously as she made the toast and the bright color shown in her cheeks and the mist-laden wind played tenderly with her dark curls.

Some Were Timid

Then two-score invited guests filed in, their faces expressing all the emotions, ranging from pleased expectancy to a very palpable timidity. Then a second car was swung to the landing and more guests piled in. Some men with voices of marked huskiness shouted unintelligible orders to each other and the great wheel began to revolve for the first time.

It was 6:32 o'clock. Slowly, almost imperceptibly, it lifted the cars away from the earth, revolving from east to west. A fourth of the way up the wheel stopped. The passengers gasped in unison and looked at each other with smiles more or less sickly. They looked down and saw that they were hanging directly over the Austrian village. Suddenly they heard the regular throbbing of the engines again and felt much better.

The wheel climbed steadily upward and the passengers grew bolder. Some of them looked over the edge of the car and at once became less bold. In eight minutes the wheel had completed the first quarter of the circle. In seven minutes more the loaded cars had measured half the circumference and hung 266 feet above the earth.

Again the engines stopped and the champagne was poured. All in the two cars drank standing to George W. S. [sic] Ferris, Mrs. Ferris proposing the toast and calling it across to those in the next car. Then all gave three cheers to the inventor and drank to the health of his pretty wife with immense enthusiasm.

Main Idea Question

1. According to the selection, what is the reason that Mrs. Ferris toasted her husband?
   A. Her husband was retiring from a long career of inventing machines.
   B. Her husband was opening a theme park.
   C. She wished him success with his new invention.
   D. The Ferris wheel brought joy to many people.

Plot Question

2. According to the article, when does the story take place?
   F. late 1800s
   G. early 1800s
   H. late 1900s
   I. early 1900s

Purpose Question

3. Which sentence best states the author's purpose for writing this article?
   A. to entertain readers with a story of how the Ferris wheel was invented
   B. to persuade readers to ride the Ferris wheel
   C. to inform of the dangers of the Ferris wheel
   D. to describe the first time experiences of people on the Ferris wheel

Main Idea Question

4. Which sentence states the most important idea in the article?
   F. She said softly as she made the toast: "To the health of my husband and the success of the Ferris wheel."
   G. Then two-score invited guests filed in, their faces expressing all the emotions, ranging from pleased expectancy to a very palpable timidity.
   H. The passengers gasped in unison and looked at each other with smiles more or less sickly.
   I. In seven minutes more the loaded cars had measured half the circumference and hung 266 feet above the earth.

Plot Question

5. Based on information in the selection, what conclusion can be drawn about Mrs. Ferris?
   A. She was embarrassed that so many people were afraid to try her husband's invention.
   B. She was proud of her husband and his invention.
   C. She was a great advertiser for the Ferris wheel.
   D. She disliked her husband's invention.

Purpose Question

6. Why does the author use the title "266 Feet in the Air"?

   F. to tell readers the circumference of the Ferris wheel
   G. to scare readers about the dangers of the Ferris wheel
   H. to explain how many people rode on the Ferris wheel
   I. to preview a detail about the Ferris wheel

Comparison/Contrast and Cause/Effect

COMMON COMPARISON/CONTRAST WORDS AND PHRASES

> Tip: Fifteen to twenty-five percent of the questions on the FCAT Reading Test will ask you to compare and contrast or to find the cause or effect.

- although
- but
- different from
- either or
- however
- in comparison
- in contrast
- on the other hand
- similarly
- still
- unless
- while
- yet

COMMON CAUSE/EFFECT WORDS AND PHRASES

- as a result
- because
- for this reason
- if . . . then
- since
- therefore
- thus

Comparison/Contrast Practice

1. Write a comparison of two sports. Use at least two examples of how these sports are similar.

_____

_____

_____

_____

_____

_____

_____

2. Contrast the two sports you compared in the above question. Use at least two examples of how these sports are different.

_____

_____

_____

_____

_____

_____

_____

Cause/Effect Practice

1. Explain why students get bad grades. Include at least two reasons why in your answer.

   _____

   _____

   _____

   _____

   _____

   _____

   _____

2. Think of someone who has influenced you and your life. Who is this person, and how has he or she influenced your character and development? Include at least four details in your answer.

   _____

   _____

   _____

   _____

   _____

   _____

   _____

Reference/Research

You will be evaluated on how well you are able to

- locate, organize, and interpret written information.
- combine information from two texts or from a text and graphic information.
- check the accuracy of research information.
- evaluate whether an argument presented in the text is weak or strong.

Tip: Ten to thirty percent of the questions will ask you to use graphs, diagrams, or charts to evaluate information presented to you.

Reference/Research Practice

Use the following charts, pictures, and maps to answer the questions that follow. You can check your answers against the suggested answers provided later in this chapter.

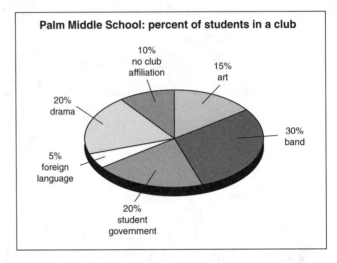

Palm Middle School: percent of students in a club

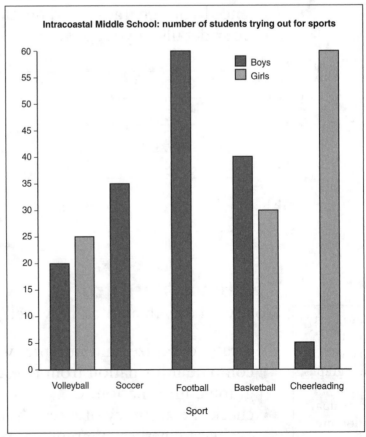

Intracoastal Middle School: number of students trying out for sports

1. Which sports are most likely to be funded by schools because of their popularity, according to the chart?

_____

_____

_____

_____

_____

_____

_____

_____

_____

_____

2. How does your school compare to the charts above? Which clubs and sports do you have at your school? And how does your school compare to the charts above?

_____

_____

_____

_____

_____

_____

_____

_____

_____

_____

_____

Review the following maps before answering the questions that follow.

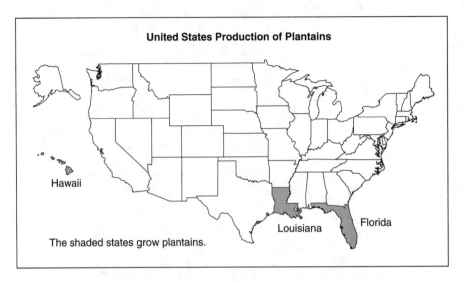

The banana is at the top, and the plantain is on the bottom. Note the differences in size, shape, stems, and color.

3. In which states are plantains probably cheaper to buy because they are grown there?

_____

_____

4. According to the picture, in what ways are bananas and plantains different?

_____

_____

_____

_____

_____

_____

_____

_____

ANSWERING SHORT-RESPONSE AND EXTENDED-RESPONSE QUESTIONS

Approximately five to seven of the questions on the FCAT Reading Test are short response or extended response. They are introduced by the phrase READ/THINK/ EXPLAIN. If you do not know the answers to these questions, don't worry! Partial credit is given for these questions, so write whatever you know. You may even include direct quotes (sentences or phrases) from the text in your answer.

Follow these basic guidelines:

Tip: Always write an answer because partial credit is given.

■ When you answer READ/THINK/EXPLAIN questions, think and organize what you want to say before writing down your ideas.
■ Write your short and long answers neatly so that anyone can read them.

Short Response

A short-response question

■ should be answered in about 5 minutes or less.
■ should be written within the eight lines allowed on the answer sheet.

■ is worth 2 points, but partial credit may be given.

■ asks you to write an example, list three reasons, or compare and contrast two techniques.

In order to get full credit, a short response must include the following:

■ a clearly written, correct answer.

■ sufficient details from the article to explain the answer.

Short-Response Practice

In response to the article on the Ferris wheel, read the following question and answer it on the lines provided. A sample answer can be found later in the chapter.

Based on the information in the selection, what assumption can be made about George W. S. [sic] Ferris? Include information from the selection to support your assumption.

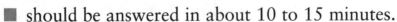

Extended Response

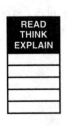

An extended-response question

■ should be answered in about 10 to 15 minutes.

■ should be written within the 14 lines allowed on the answer sheet.

■ is worth 4 points, but partial credit may be given.

■ asks you to compare and contrast, explain cause and effects, or give three or more details to explain something.

In order to get full credit, an extended response must include the following:

▪ a clearly written, correct answer.
▪ sufficient details from the article to explain the answer.

Extended-Response Practice

In response to the article on the Ferris wheel, read the following question and answer it on the lines provided. A sample answer can be found later in the chapter.

Was Mr. Ferris's invention a good idea? Provide four details from the selection to support your answer.

_____

_____

_____

_____

_____

_____

_____

_____

_____

_____

_____

_____

_____

_____

_____

_____

_____

_____

PRACTICE TEST

Note: This is not a complete reading test—two complete practice tests can be found at the end of this book.

~The Bill of Rights~

Bill of Rights

Amendment I
Congress shall make no law respecting an establishment of religion, or prohibiting the free exercise thereof; or abridging the freedom of speech, or of the press; or the right of the people peaceably to assemble, and to petition the government for a redress of grievances.

Amendment II
A well regulated militia, being necessary to the security of a free state, the right of the people to keep and bear arms, shall not be infringed.

Amendment III
No soldier shall, in time of peace be quartered in any house, without the consent of the owner, nor in time of war, but in a manner to be prescribed by law.

Amendment IV
The right of the people to be secure in their persons, houses, papers, and effects, against unreasonable searches and seizures, shall not be violated, and no warrants shall issue, but upon probable cause, supported by oath or affirmation, and particularly describing the place to be searched, and the persons or things to be seized.

Amendment V

No person shall be held to answer for a capital, or otherwise infamous crime, unless on a presentment or indictment of a grand jury, except in cases arising in the land or naval forces, or in the militia, when in actual service in time of war or public danger; nor shall any person be subject for the same offense to be twice put in jeopardy of life or limb; nor shall be compelled in any criminal case to be a witness against himself, nor be deprived of life, liberty, or property, without due process of law; nor shall private property be taken for public use, without just compensation.

Amendment VI

In all criminal prosecutions, the accused shall enjoy the right to a speedy and public trial, by an impartial jury of the state and district wherein the crime shall have been committed, which district shall have been previously ascertained by law, and to be informed of the nature and cause of the accusation; to be confronted with the witnesses against him; to have compulsory process for obtaining witnesses in his favor, and to have the assistance of counsel for his defense.

Amendment VII

In suits at common law, where the value in controversy shall exceed twenty dollars, the right of trial by jury shall be preserved, and no fact tried by a jury, shall be otherwise reexamined in any court of the United States, than according to the rules of the common law.

Amendment VIII

Excessive bail shall not be required, nor excessive fines imposed, nor cruel and unusual punishments inflicted.

Amendment IX

The enumeration in the Constitution, of certain rights, shall not be construed to deny or disparage others retained by the people.

Amendment X

The powers not delegated to the United States by the Constitution, nor prohibited by it to the states, are reserved to the states respectively, or to the people.

1. In the First Amendment, what does the word "prohibiting" mean?
   A. allowing
   B. restricting
   C. contrasting
   D. receiving

2. Which amendment allows us to confront our accusers?
   F. Amendment I
   G. Amendment III
   H. Amendment V
   I. Amendment VI

3. The first ten amendments are called the Bill of Rights because
   A. they list basic rights that we all are promised as U.S. citizens.
   B. they are like a price that was paid for our freedom.
   C. they announce our status to other countries.
   D. they protect us from having to pay for our freedoms.

READ
THINK
EXPLAIN

4. READ/THINK/EXPLAIN: What basic rights affect you today? Use details and examples from the story in your answer.

_____

_____

_____

_____

_____

_____

_____

A Survivor's Hope

Waiting and wondering,
hoping and praying,
wanting to be free again,
but never knowing when.

First they came for my neighbors,
then they came for us, too.
Now I share my bed with five others,
and my food with only three.

We didn't have a plan,
and we lost hope
as our captors neglected us.
But today I saw an eagle soar above the camp,
and I've regained my hope.

That single bird
has renewed my faith in freedom.
and my hope has been restored.

Again, we wait and wonder,
hope and pray, until our liberators
set us free.

Another year has passed. . . .
1944 did not bring freedom,
but I have hope for 1945.

5. The author's purpose is
   F. to persuade the reader to be positive.
   G. to explain how the author kept hope during a difficult time.
   H. to describe what it was like to live through the Holocaust.
   I. to inform the reader of the author's life story.

6. The liberators to which the author refers are probably
   A. the group fighting the Nazis.
   B. a group of criminals.
   C. the police.
   D. the people running the concentration camp.

7. READ/THINK/EXPLAIN: What did the author probably survive? Use details and examples from the text to support your answer.

_____

_____

_____

_____

_____

_____

_____

_____

_____

Healthy Teeth and Gums Are up to You

Gum disease can be prevented with good brushing and flossing habits. It's important that you pay attention to your teeth.

Think of your teeth as fine china. Would your mother use a rough, metal scouring pad to clean her priceless dishes? No. In the same way, you should not use hard bristled toothbrushes to brush your teeth.

Replace your toothbrush every three to four months unless your toothbrush is rough. In that case, replace it sooner so that it doesn't damage your gums.

Instructions on Brushing Teeth Properly
Step One: Place your toothbrush along your gums at an angle. The bristles of the brush should touch both your gums and your teeth.

Step Two: Brushing two to three teeth at a time, gently brush your teeth using circular motions. Continue until all teeth have been brushed.
Step Three: Using a back-and-forth motion, brush the biting surfaces of your teeth.

8. According to the article, brushing your teeth with a hard bristle can cause
   F. cuts and scrapes on the surface of your teeth.
   G. cavities.
   H. gum disease.
   I. gingivitis.

9. It's time to replace your toothbrush when
   A. it's been three to four months.
   B. the bristles are hard.
   C. the bristles are broken.
   D. all of the above

10. Another title for this article could be
    F. "Healthy Brushing Habits."
    G. "When to Buy a New Toothbrush."
    H. "Why a Hard Bristle Is Bad."
    I. "Soft Bristles Are Good."

TIPS FOR PARENTS

■ The best advice for all students taking the FCAT Reading Test is to read, read, and read some more! As a parent, encourage your child to read all different types of books and literature but keep in mind that more than half of the passages on the FCAT Reading Test are nonfiction.

■ Subscribe to educational magazines like *National Geographic* and also subscribe to music or sports magazines that are of interest to teenagers.

■ Play games as a family that promote good vocabulary skills like charades, Pictionary, and Balderdash.

■ Ask your child questions about what he or she has read. It's always better to ask this shortly after he or she has finished reading.

■ Go to the library with your child.

TIPS FOR TEACHERS

■ Watch a movie after your students finish reading a novel. Discuss what was different about the movie compared to what happened in the novel. Make a T-chart on the board.

■ Allow silent reading time once a week for 20 minutes.

■ Require students to turn in a reading log with a minimum of 1 hour per week. Count it as a homework grade. Make sure your students are reading books at their appropriate levels and challenge them, from time to time, to read above that level.

■ Have a "word of the day" that is at or above grade level. Encourage the students to use the words in homework assignments, essays, discussions, and so on.

■ Teach root words, prefixes, and suffixes. Knowing these important skills will enable your students to decipher difficult vocabulary words they encounter on the test.

■ Have students keep a journal while reading.

- Require short-answer questions on tests instead of using all multiple-choice questions.
- Another way to help students with the short-answer questions is to give them a true/false test, but they must explain their answer in one or two sentences for full credit.
- Use graphic organizers like story maps, Venn diagrams, flow charts, plot lines, and so on.

ANSWERS

Reading Practice

Some Were Timid

Then two-score invited guests filed in, their faces expressing all the emotions, ranging from pleased expectancy to a very palpable timidity. Then a second car was swung to the landing and more guests piled in. Some men with voices of marked huskiness shouted unintelligible orders to each other and the great wheel began to revolve for the first time.

It was 6:32 o'clock. Slowly, almost imperceptibly, it lifted the cars away from the earth, revolving from east to west. A fourth of the way up the wheel stopped. The passengers gasped in unison and looked at each other with smiles more or less sickly. They looked down and saw that they were hanging directly over the Austrian village. Suddenly they heard the regular throbbing of the engines again and felt much better.

The wheel climbed steadily upward and the passengers grew bolder. Some of them looked over the edge of the car and at once became less bold. In eight minutes the wheel had completed the first quarter of the circle. In seven minutes more the loaded cars had measured half the circumference and hung 266 feet above the earth.

Again the engines stopped and the champagne was poured. All in the two cars drank standing to George W. S. [sic] Ferris, Mrs. Ferris proposing the toast and calling it across to those in the next car. Then all gave three cheers to the inventor and drank to the health of his pretty wife with immense enthusiasm.

Summary: This is the description of the first time the Ferris wheel carried people on a ride.

Vocabulary Practice

1. The correct answer is A (small).
2. The correct answer is G (great).
3. The correct answer is D (breathed in air with shock).
4. The correct answer is H (not able to be understood).
5. The correct answer is B (beating).

Main Idea/Plot/Purpose Practice

1. The correct answer is C (because she wished him success for his new invention).
2. The correct answer is F (late 1800s).
3. The correct answer is D (to describe the first time experience of people on the Ferris wheel).
4. The correct answer is F (She said softly as she made the toast: "To the health. . . .").
5. The correct answer is B (She was proud of her husband and his invention).
6. The correct answer is I (to preview a detail about the Ferris wheel).

Comparison/Contrast Practice

Note: Answers will vary.

Cause/Effect Practice

Note: Answers will vary.

Reference/Research Practice

1. The correct answer should include football, basketball, and cheerleading.
2. *Note:* Answers will vary.
3. The correct answer is *bananas*.
4. The correct answer should include texture, size, uses (in recipes).

Short-Response Practice

A 2-point response should include some of the following:

- creative
- inventor
- enjoyed amusement parks
- highly respected
- brought joy to many people around the world

Extended-Response Practice

A 4-point response should include

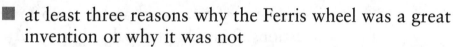

- at least three reasons why the Ferris wheel was a great invention or why it was not
- examples from the story supporting the opinion

Practice Test

1. The correct answer is B (restricting).
2. The correct answer is I (Amendment VI).
3. The correct answer is A (They list the basic rights that we all are promised as U.S. citizens).
4. *Note*: Answers will vary.
5. The correct answer is G (to explain how she kept hope during a difficult time).
6. The correct answer is A (the group fighting the Nazis).
7. *Note*: Answers will vary.
8. The correct answer is H (gum disease).
9. The correct answer is D (all of the above)
10. The correct answer is F (Healthy Brushing Habits).

Chapter 3

Taking the FCAT Writing+ Test (Essay)

Each February, the FCAT Writing+ Test is given. This test is made up of one essay and 45 to 50 multiple-choice questions. This chapter will guide you through preparation for the essay portion of the test.

According to the FCAT web site, your essay will be scored by two "trained readers [mostly teachers and former teachers] using the holistic method." What this means is that your essay will be evaluated on its overall quality. The readers will consider four elements when looking at your essay: focus, organization, support, and conventions. (You'll find these terms in the vocabulary list later in this chapter.) The benefit for you is that the people reading and scoring your essay will not focus on only one part of your essay for the final score. The two readers' scores for your essay will be averaged to give you a final score between 1 and 6, with 6 being a "perfect" score. For example, one evaluator gives your essay a 4, but the other evaluator gives you a 5. To determine your score, add 4 and 5 together to get 9 and then divide by 2. With these two scores, you would earn an averaged score of 4.5. (Other possible scores are 1, 1.5, 2, 2.5, and so on.)

Throughout this chapter, you will study the four elements: focus, organization, support, and conventions. Each element will be explained, and examples will be presented. Then, you will focus in on the two types of essays: expository and persuasive. More specific information will be given to help you prepare for each type of prompt.

> Tip: You will be allowed 45 minutes for this test. Budget your time wisely so that you have enough time to actually write and edit your paper.

Finally, you will be asked to practice writing an essay, step by step. Take the time to read the information presented and to study each example before practicing. Once you have completed all four elements and have learned about both expository and persuasive writing, you will be asked to practice writing an essay from start to finish.

FOCUS

Tip: In order to maintain focus, stick to one main idea in your essay.

The reader of your essay expects you to clearly present one main idea; this is your focus. This part of the essay process should take no longer than 5 minutes. You must practice the steps in this section until you are comfortable completing them quickly. The only way the reader of your essay will be able to judge your effectiveness in the area of focus is in the actual essay itself, as he or she will not see any of the brainstorming that preceded your writing.

Any information that does not support your main idea is extra information and breaks your focus. Study the following examples:

Prompt: Write an expository essay about whether or not you like classical music.

Focused thesis statement: My favorite type of music is classical because it helps me to relax while I study for a test. (This thesis clearly answers the prompt by explaining why the student likes classical music.)

Off-topic thesis statement: I like rap music because it is fun to dance to. (This thesis statement does not mention classical music at all and would result in an unscorable essay.)

In order to score well on your essay in regard to focus, you must carefully read the prompt. As soon as you receive your test paper, read the "Writing Situation" and the "Directions for Writing." Your prompt will be either expository or persuasive, so you must prepare for both because you won't know in advance which one you will be given. The writing situation is the topic you have been given, and the directions for writing tell you how to focus your topic.

ORGANIZATION

Before you begin writing, you should spend about 5 minutes organizing your thoughts so that you have a clear beginning, middle, and end to your essay. Also, arrange your ideas in a logical way so that they make sense. You wouldn't write about the time you learned to ride a bike and start by describing how you fell off for the *third* time, would you? Another aspect of organization is to make sure that when you change ideas from paragraph to paragraph, the reader is not left wondering how you got to the next point. Use transitions to unify your ideas and create a sense of order. Finally, a good summary of your paper with a strong concluding sentence will guarantee you a better score.

Tip: For a list of transitions, see page 52 at the end of the section on support.

Brainstorm

After you choose your focus, begin brainstorming by listing ideas about that one main topic. Brainstorming is an important step when writing an essay. Listing many ideas in a short amount of time may spark some details that you can add to your finished essay. It is much easier to look at a list of ideas than at a blank sheet!

What exactly is brainstorming? Brainstorming is writing down anything—words or phrases—that have to do with your topic. Avoid writing sentences because this will take too long. You may or may not use everything you have brainstormed. This is a time to write everything that comes to mind when you read your topic. The less you write, the faster this step will go. One way to save time when brainstorming is to actually do your brainstorming using a graphic organizer like a web. The next section on planning will explain how to do this. (See the appendix for more graphic organizers. Choose the one you like best and use it when you plan your writing.)

Plan

If you take the time to organize your brainstorming, your ideas will naturally be better developed in your essay. However, it is important to remember that neither your planning nor your brainstorming will be graded. You should not spend more than 5 minutes on these two steps, and do your writing only on the planning sheet provided.

What exactly is planning? There are many ways to plan your essay, but the two most popular are webbing and outlining. Webbing looks like a spider's web because it consists of circles enclosing your main points and smaller circles connected with the elaboration to support your points. This can also be called clustering. Outlining is more formal and is generally used when writing a research paper. Practice both methods to determine which is most comfortable for you; then use that method the day of the test.

OUTLINING

Tip: See page 57 for an example of an effective expository outline.

One way to organize your brainstorming is to write an informal outline. First, look at your brainstorming list of words and phrases. A basic guideline for your outline is to write between four and six Roman numerals (one for each paragraph you will write). What you write next to the Roman numerals does not have to be complete sentences, but just enough information to prompt you to write. If you cannot create an informal outline in less than 5 minutes, this method of organization is not recommended for planning and organizing your essay.

For a five-paragraph essay:

■ The first Roman numeral briefly introduces your essay. This paragraph clearly states your topic and gives a quick overview of your main points. You need not give the details or examples of each of your points, just briefly state them with interest.

■ The second, third, and fourth Roman numerals discuss your main points or reasons. In each paragraph, write a topic sentence for that main point and discuss *only* that main point. Beneath these Roman numerals, give at least two examples of your point by indenting and labeling them with capital letters.

■ The fifth Roman numeral concludes your topic. Never give new information in your conclusion. All your points must already have been made. This is simply the time to summarize your points and give one last statement to make an impression on the reader.

WEBBING (ALSO KNOWN AS MAPPING OR CLUSTERING)

A quicker way to organize your brainstorming is to draw a "web" or "map" of your ideas. This is the most flexible method because it allows you to add ideas easily without changing numbers or letters. First, place the subject of the essay in the middle and draw a bubble around it. Then, draw a line outward for each main point that will be covered in the essay. From these main points, you can then add the supporting details by drawing lines from the point to its detail. This method also allows you to determine the order of your ideas. Do not write complete sentences in the bubbles; keep your writing to a minimum to save time for the actual writing of the essay. (See the appendix for more examples of graphic organizers.)

For a five paragraph essay, your web would look something like this:

General Student Web

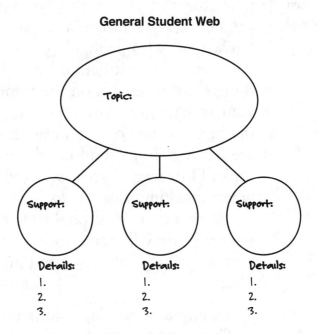

It is important to note that there are many other methods of organizing your prewriting. Remember to check the appendix for other graphic organizers and practice them. Use the one you find most comfortable and that allows you to work the fastest.

SUPPORT

The third element the reader of your essay will consider is how well you have supported your thesis (main idea). Have you explained, clarified, or defined each point? To do the best job in this area, you must use good vocabulary, be specific with your nouns (avoid words like "things" or "stuff"), and make your explanations complete. Overall, make your points clear and easy to understand, but be specific and detailed when doing so. Because this is the actual part that will be graded, you should spend the majority of your time on this step.

Tip: Use detailed adjectives and specific nouns when describing in your essay.

It is important that the reader connects with you and with what you've written. In order to achieve this important aspect of your essay, you must remember that you are presenting your information to someone who doesn't know you, who probably doesn't know anything about what you are writing, and who has read hundreds, maybe thousands, of essays on the same topic. Therefore, explain your statements thoroughly but be creative; think "out of the box" when coming up with your support. Imagine you are really telling an adult what you believe about your topic. However, if you use slang or improper grammar when speaking, do not do so in your essay. If you are able to create a conversational tone that captures the reader, your writing will come to life with an effective tone, and your score will increase, too! Study the following examples:

> Example of writing that is unclear:
> **Gwazi was good, but Montu was the best.**

> Example of writing that is clear:
> **The wooden roller coaster, Gwazi, had a lot of jerks and turns that kept me on the edge of my seat. But I really loved the way Montu kept my feet dangling below me, scaring me around every loop!**

In order to score well on your essay in regard to support, you must include three main parts in your essay: the introduction, the body, and the conclusion. The following information will guide you through this process.

Writing the Essay

Tip: Write your main points clearly in each part of your outline, web, or other graphic device.

Now you can turn your planning (your outline, web, or map) into an essay with paragraphs. It will be much easier for you to begin writing your essay now that you have your ideas organized on paper. If you have written an outline, write a paragraph for each Roman numeral. If you have created a web or map, write a paragraph for each bubble.

The *introduction* should be brief. You must have a thesis statement that clearly states your topic or point of view and ties your entire essay together. This sentence is considered a "hook" that captures the reader's attention and makes him or her want to read the rest of the essay. You can place this sentence at the beginning or the end of your introductory paragraph. To support your thesis, write two or three sentences that summarize the main points to be presented in your essay. Keep this paragraph interesting; do not just simply list your information. Remember, this is what will catch the reader's attention and will set your essay apart from the thousands of others.

■ Types of hooks include a fact, an anecdote, a direction, a question, a quotation, or an exclamatory sentence.

The *body paragraphs* give support and elaboration to your thesis statement. In approximately three paragraphs, the body is what proves your point. In order for you to score well, each paragraph should have a topic sentence for one main idea along with several elaborating detail sentences. Like the thesis, the topic sentence can be placed at the beginning or the end of the paragraph, whichever makes the point more clear. Write about only one point or one reason in each paragraph. Keep these paragraphs organized in a logical manner. Use transition words and phrases like "my next point" or "in addition to" within paragraphs as well as between paragraphs (see the list of common transitions at the end of this section). Make your details jump off the page by using words related to the five senses. The more your reader can experience what you are explaining, the more convincing you will be. Your body paragraphs should be filled with examples of the topic sentence. This is the time to use vivid words. And finally, include any statistics or facts related to your topic for further proof of your thesis.

■ Types of elaboration to include in your body paragraphs include facts, statistics, sensory details, vivid imagery, incidents, examples, and quotations.

The *conclusion* never brings up new information in the essay. If it does, it is no longer the conclusion but another body paragraph. This paragraph clearly restates your main idea in a way that the reader will remember it or in a way that will move the reader to want to do something about what you have written. In an expository essay, this is known as the "clincher" statement. This last statement presents the main idea in a way that makes your point dramatically. In a persuasive essay, the last statement is known as the "call to action." This "call" urges the reader to actually take action in response to your main point.

> Tip: Pay attention to the news, magazines, and especially to your teachers. You will be able to use the facts, statistics, and details from these sources in your essay as support.

Catching the Reader's Attention with a Strong "Hook"

In order to catch your reader's attention and draw him or her into your essay, you must write an effective "hook." This is the statement that introduces your topic in a unique way and sets your essay apart from the thousands of others on the same topic.

Avoid starting your essay in the following manner:

My favorite _____ is . . . .
My opinion on _____ is . . . .

Example
Read the following topic and the hooks that follow.

Topic: Favorite author.

Noneffective hook: My favorite author is Mark Twain because he writes about adventure.

Effective hook: Adventures that take me rafting down the Mississippi River, bunking with thieves, and escaping with a runaway slave make Mark Twain my favorite author.

Practice

Below are five topics. For each topic, write a sentence that captures the reader's attention and at the same time introduces your main idea or thesis.

1. *Topic*: My favorite meal.
Hook: _____

2. *Topic*: Why music CDs should have parental warnings.
Hook: _____

3. *Topic*: The causes of beach erosion.
Hook: _____

4. *Topic*: Why students must have electives in addition to academic classes.
Hook: _____

5. *Topic*: The best teacher I ever had.
Hook: _____

Review the essays you've written so far and add a hook to each introduction if you do not already have one. You'll find it is actually fun to come up with the one sentence that will make your essay different from everyone else's.

Strengthening the Essay with Figurative Language

To make your writing come alive for the reader, you must learn how to effectively use figurative language in your essay. Figurative language is more descriptive and takes your essay from boring to interesting.

Look back over the essays you have written in this chapter. You can make them even more interesting, and possibly increase your potential score, by adding figurative language. Figurative language includes metaphors, similes, personification, and imagery.

A *metaphor* is a comparison that does not use the word "like" or "as."

Example: Sarah is a walking dictionary. (Sarah is being compared to a dictionary without using "like" or "as.")

Practice

In sentence form, create metaphors with the following nouns. (Suggested answers can be found at the end of this chapter.)

1. cat
2. uncle
3. school
4. breakfast
5. grass

A *simile* is a comparison using "like" or "as."

Example: The city looked like a patchwork quilt from the airplane. (The city is compared to a quilt using "like.")

Practice

Use the following nouns to create sentences that are metaphors. (Suggested answers can be found at the end of this chapter.)

1. dog
2. house
3. car
4. street
5. book

Personification gives human qualities to something that is not human. This technique provides a more vivid picture of what the object looks like or what the object is doing.

Example: The willow tree branches danced in the wind.

Dancing is an action that people perform, not tree branches. But use of the verb "danced" gives the reader a more vivid picture of *how* the tree's branches moved.

Practice

Personify the underlined (nonhuman) nouns in the following sentences. Change the words in parentheses to words that could describe a human's actions. (Suggested answers can be found at the end of this chapter.)

1. The garage <u>door</u> (closed).
2. The <u>kitten</u> (meowed) when I left for school.
3. The bathroom <u>light</u> (went off).
4. My <u>hat</u> (is) on my head.
5. The <u>airplane</u> (took off).

Imagery uses the five senses (sight, smell, touch, sound, taste) to create vivid descriptions.

Example: The dark purple, thundering clouds brought forth stinging rain that tasted salty as I stuck out my tongue to taste it. (Sight words are "dark" and "purple"; taste is represented by "salty"; the sound is that of "thunder"; and touch is represented by the word "stinging.")

More examples of imagery are listed in the following chart. Complete the chart with more examples of your own.

Sense	Example
Sight	Colors, cracked, shiny
Smell	Fishy, chocolate chip cookies
Touch	Sticky, prickly
Sound	Drum beats, high-pitched
Taste	Sweet, sour

Practice

Rewrite each sentence below including images using the sense indicated in italics. (Suggested answers can be found at the end of this chapter.)

1. I love to watch the waves at the beach—*sight*.
2. My favorite game is soccer—*touch*.
3. My mom's cooking tastes great—*taste*.
4. Band practice is noisy—*sound*.
5. Thanksgiving dinner smells—*smell*.

Using Words above Grade Level

It has been mentioned that you will improve your score if you use words above your grade level, even if you don't know how to spell them. Here are 15 words from a tenth-grade vocabulary list that you should review and try to include in your essay. Remember, even if you forget the correct spelling, using these words correctly in your essay will improve your score.

After you study these words, look up 15 new vocabulary words in the dictionary and write them on the lines provided. The more new words you are able to learn and put to use, the more likely you are to use them on the test. A really great way to add these words to your working vocabulary is to try to use each one at least three times. Just pick one word per day and try to find three different, appropriate times to use it. Before you know it, you will have increased your vocabulary in just one or two months.

Another way to improve your vocabulary is to write vocabulary words on flashcards. Keep them in a stack with a rubber band. Carry them around with you and quiz yourself often. You will be amazed at how quickly these words will become part of your personal vocabulary.

> Tip: Using higher-level vocabulary in your essay, even if you misspell the word, can actually improve your score.

Vocabulary List

1. serendipity—luck in making unexpected and fortunate discoveries
2. unfathomable—unthinkable or unable to be understood
3. fallible—likely to make a mistake or error
4. vehement—passionate about something (usually in a negative way)
5. proficient—skilled or qualified in a particular area
6. chronic—lasting a long time
7. desolate—without people; without joy
8. diligent—hard-working
9. ostracize—to exclude from society
10. ambivalence—opposing emotional attitudes (for example, love and hate) toward the same object
11. amiable—friendly
12. dissuade—to persuasively prevent someone from doing something
13. intrinsic—coming from within
14. flippant—frivolous
15. authoritarian—one who enforces authority or expects unquestioned obedience
16. _____
17. _____
18. _____
19. _____
20. _____
21. _____
22. _____
23. _____
24. _____
25. _____
26. _____
27. _____
28. _____
29. _____
30. _____

Practice

In each sentence, replace the underlined word(s) with a word from the vocabulary list above. You may need to rewrite some of the sentences. (Suggested answers can be found at the end of this chapter.)

1. The cafeteria was <u>empty</u> after lunch.
2. My grandmother's disease <u>lasted a long time</u>.
3. Many people tell me that I am <u>friendly</u>.
4. Even though my teacher is very intelligent, she can still be <u>wrong</u> about current trends!
5. I want to <u>keep</u> my principal from banning cell phones at school.

Using Transitions

In order to create a natural transition between ideas and paragraphs, you must use effective transitions. Here are some of the most common and useful transitions:

Tip: Transitions are key to an essay's organization.

additionally	consequently	however	next
after	despite	in addition to	second
again	earlier	in conclusion	similarly
also	first	in contrast	then
although	for example	in other words	therefore
as a result	for instance	in summary	until
as soon as	furthermore	last	when
before			

CONVENTIONS

Now that you have written your essay, take a look at the conventions, or the writing skills you have displayed in your paragraphs. The reader of your essay is looking for correct punctuation, capitalization, and spelling, as well as sentences that are varied in their structure. With even a few minor mistakes, you can still earn a "perfect" score of 6. However, many mistakes in this area could bring your score down a whole point or two. It is hoped that you have saved at least 5 minutes for this important step.

In order to score well on your essay in regard to conventions, you must follow two basic guidelines: proofread and edit your essay.

What's the difference between proofreading and editing? *Proofreading* involves looking for mistakes; *editing* involves making your essay better in some way. Always leave yourself at least several minutes for this critical step. Without proofreading and editing your essay, you could actually lose a point in scoring. It is acceptable for you to cross out words that you want to delete and insert words that you want to add—just do so neatly. If you have more than 5 minutes left at this stage, reread your essay and edit it until the time is up. Make sure your paper is as perfect as possible!

Here are some questions to ask yourself when proofreading and editing your essay:

> Tip: Proofreading is correcting mistakes. Editing is rewriting for clarity.

Proofreading:
- Have you made any obvious spelling errors?
- Have you capitalized all proper nouns? Have you capitalized the first word of each sentence?
- Is each sentence complete with a subject and a verb?
- Does each sentence have correct punctuation?

Editing:
- Is there a more challenging vocabulary word you could substitute for a simple one? (Even if you are unsure of the spelling of a better word, use it.)
- Have you used vague words like "thing," "stuff," "good," or "fun"? Replace each of those words with a more specific noun or adjective.
- Do your sentences all begin the same way? If so, change them around a little. (Try starting a sentence with an adverb.)
- Have you used too many forms of "to be" in your essay? If so, replace them with more active verbs. (Active verbs include "run," "leap," "mesmerize," "laugh," "smell," and so on.)

Proofreading and Editing Practice

Proofreading Directions: Proofread the following sentences for spelling, capitalization, and punctuation. Rewrite each sentence correctly on the line given. (Answers can be found at the end of this chapter.)

1. Remember to look at you're notes before you take the test.

   _____

2. When I heard dad call my name, I knew I had been caught.

   _____

3. Every time I want to walk my dog the rain starts to pour.

   _____

4. Their are many people in the world who do not understand the meaning of peace.

   _____

5. When will you be available to study with me for the big test.

   _____

6. Mom went to the grocery store but she forgot her checkbook.

   _____

7. I have alot of homework tonight.

   _____

8. In an outline, use Roman numerals to indicate your major headings.

   _____

9. Werent you in my first period class, too?

   _____

10. Have you read the book <u>animal farm</u>?

    _____

Editing Directions: Rewrite the following sentences on the line given, improving the sentence structure, vocabulary/word choice, and active verbs as noted in parentheses. (Note: There is more than one correct way to rewrite many of these sentences.)

11. One thing about my teacher that I like is that she takes the time to listen to my questions. (*word choice*)

    _____

12. Tommy, my classmate, is great at everything he does. (*verb, word choice*)

    _____

13. Sally plays in the school band. Sally sings in the choir, too. (*sentence structure*)

    _____

14. How much stuff is in your backpack? (*word choice*)

    _____

15. Jamal is a hard worker. (*verb*)

    _____

16. My sister is not an honest person. (*verb*)

    _____

17. There are many reasons why I love summer. (*sentence structure*)

    _____

18. Everything in my locker started to smell because I left my lunch in there over the weekend. (*word choice*)

    _____

19. I will return your video game after school. (*sentence structure*)

    _____

20. My friend John will be the best soccer player on the team. (*verb*)

    _____

THE EXPOSITORY ESSAY

Focus
READING AND UNDERSTANDING THE EXPOSITORY PROMPT

Tip: An expository essay *explains*.

An *expository prompt* is a topic that describes someone or something to the reader. Often the writing situation is a topic that asks you to explain why or how, clarify a process, or define a concept. Sometimes the topic asks you to write about a person or idea. One way to prepare for the expository essay is to thumb through scrapbooks or old photo albums and ask your parents for stories about the people in the photos. Thinking about your own childhood memories will provide many topics that would be appropriate for the expository essay. Key words that tell you the prompt is expository include "explain" and "elaborate."

Example

Writing Situation: *Everyone has a hero, someone they admire.*

Directions for Writing: *Before you begin writing, think about who your hero is and why. Then explain why this person is your hero.*

CHOOSING A FOCUS FOR THE EXPOSITORY ESSAY

First you must decide which person, place, or thing you will write about. List a few topics that come to mind. Then circle *one* and begin the next step, brainstorming.

Example

For the writing situation "Everyone has a hero" you can write about the following possible subjects: your dad, the president, Superman, and so on. Decide which person you really believe is your hero. Make sure you choose someone you know a lot about or have strong reasons why he or she is your hero. If that person is your dad, then circle "my dad" and move on to brainstorming.

BRAINSTORMING

Remember to be brief when brainstorming. Just spend a couple of minutes writing down any details, facts, or statistics that will support the thesis you have chosen for your expository essay.

Example

My dad is my hero.

Brainstorming: tells truth, sacrifices, marines, overseas, loves me, loves mom, never complains, always puts others first, trophies, awards, honest, never lies, loves Superman, baseball team, serves, fights enemy, touchdown, letters home

Organization

Choose the method you prefer for organizing your essay. Again, spend only a short amount of time on this step, as the reader will not see this part of your essay writing.

Example

I.   *My dad is my hero. (Introduction)*
II. *My dad plays sports very well. (Reason 1)*
   A. *many trophies and awards from school*
   B. *winning touchdown in high school*
   C. *pitched strikeout in baseball*
III. *He never lies. (Reason 2)*
   A. *gave back change to a cashier*
   B. *not many honest people today*
IV. *He is brave. (Reason 3)*
   A. *sergeant in Marines*
   B. *writes me letters about war*
V.   *My dad is more than just my hero. (Conclusion)*

Support

The following is an example of an expository essay. All three main components of the essay have been listed and labeled. Read through the example, noting the thesis, the transitions used, the figurative language, and the conventions followed. Your expository essay should connect the reader to your explanation as best as possible.

Introduction

My dad is Superman! OK, so he doesn't leap tall buildings in a single bound, but he definitely has some of Superman's other qualities. I believe my dad is the most honest, hardworking man I know. He excels in everything he does, and he doesn't complain when he has difficult work. I want to be just like my dad when I grow up. My dad really is my very own Superman.

Body Paragraphs

First of all, my dad is my hero because he seems to have the talent of Superman. He plays sports like a machine. On our bookshelves, he has numerous trophies and awards from when he was in school. He played on his school's football and baseball teams. Mom tells me stories about when Dad made the winning touchdown. He was her school's hero that night. And Grandpa loves to tell the story about when Dad pitched three strikes in a row to the last player in the last inning of the championship game. Today, my dad plays on our church's softball team. Many of the other players look up to him because he plays so well and treats them with respect. So many times, people tell me that my dad is their hero, too!

Another superhero quality about my dad is that I have never heard him lie to anyone. I don't know many honest people today. For example, when I was in the third grade, I remember going to the corner store with my dad. He bought us each a soda, but the cashier gave him too much change back. My dad very honestly replied, "Excuse me, ma'am, but you only owe me fifty cents in change, not seventy-five." Wow! I was so impressed by my dad's honesty. I want to be just like him.

Right now, my dad is serving overseas as a sergeant in the Marine Corps. He serves his country without fear as he fights the enemy every day. I love to sit in bed and read the letters he writes me. My favorite letter tells a story about when he lived in a hole in the desert, waiting for the enemy for a whole week. He said he was not scared because he knew that his fellow marines were there to back him up. I do not think I could be that brave. Move over Superman, because my dad is America's hero now!

Conclusion

In conclusion, my dad's athletic talent, honesty, and bravery encourage and inspire me every day. But my dad is not just my hero; he is everyone's hero. And I really do not mind sharing my superhero Dad with my country.

PRACTICE WRITING THE EXPOSITORY ESSAY

Now, you will take what you have learned and put it into practice. Go through all of the steps outlined in this chapter before you begin writing each essay. Do not forget to write down the time you begin reading the prompt and also record the time you finish writing your essay. When writing your essay, try to budget your time wisely for each of the four steps. Recording the time you spend on your essay will give you a guideline for how long it will take you on the big day.

Expository Prompt Practice

Writing Situation: *Everyone has thought about trips they might take and places they would like to visit.*

Directions for Writing: *Think about where you would go if you could go anywhere in the world that you wanted. Now to explain in writing why you would like to visit this place.*

Time: _____

Planning Page (This page will *not* be scored. Any information you write in this section will not be considered.)

Begin your essay here:

_____

_____

_____

_____

_____

_____

_____

_____

_____

_____

_____

_____

_____

_____

_____

_____

_____

_____

_____

_____

_____

_____

_____

_____

_____

_____

_____

_____

_____

_____

_____

_____

_____

_____

_____

_____

_____

_____

_____

_____

_____

_____

_____

THE PERSUASIVE ESSAY

Tip: A persuasive essay *persuades*.

Focus

READING AND UNDERSTANDING THE PERSUASIVE PROMPT

A *persuasive prompt* is a topic that persuades the intended audience to believe your point of view and/or take a specific action. This is a topic that you would be familiar with at your age and that would not need to be researched. The directions for writing usually give you a specific audience (sometimes just one person) whom you must convince to take action. In order to prepare for the persuasive essay, pay attention to the news and to discussions in class. Also, talk to your parents about what is going on at school. Social issues that you face every day are likely to show up as a persuasive prompt. For example, you may be asked to write about cafeteria food or views about chewing gum in school. Key words that tell you the prompt is persuasive include "convince," and "persuade."

Example

Writing Situation: *The principal of your school has been asked to discuss with a parent group the possibility of a school-wide uniform policy.*

Directions for Writing: *Think about the effects a school-wide uniform policy would have on you and your friends. Now convince your principal in writing to accept your point of view on whether or not to establish a school-wide uniform policy.*

CHOOSING A FOCUS FOR THE PERSUASIVE ESSAY

First you must determine the side of the issue for which you have the most support. You should not write about both sides of an issue, as this is confusing and makes a weak argument for your position. Now begin the next step, brainstorming.

Example

For the writing situation "school-wide uniforms," you should simply decide which side of the issue you support. If you choose to be in favor of uniforms, write "for uniforms" and move on to brainstorming. Or, if you think of more reasons why the school should have a uniform policy, even if you do not agree, consider taking this side, then move on to brainstorming.

BRAINSTORMING

Remember to be brief when brainstorming. Just spend a couple of minutes writing down any details, facts, or statistics that support the thesis you have chosen for your expository essay.

Example

I am in favor of a school-wide uniform policy.

Brainstorming: *cheaper, only a few outfits needed, saves money, easier, saves time getting ready, no worry of not being in style, everyone equal, moms will be happy, less time on dress code violations/questions, easy to tell if someone's out of dress code*

Organization

Choose the method you prefer for organizing your essay. Again, spend only a short amount of time on this step, as the reader will not see this part of your essay writing.

Example

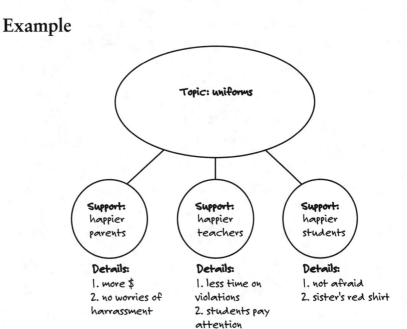

Support

The following is an example of a persuasive essay. All three main components of the essay have been listed and labeled. Read through the example, noting the thesis, the transitions used, the figurative language, and the conventions followed. Your persuasive essay should convince the reader to take action on your position.

Introduction

Personally, I hate spending time in the morning trying to figure out what to wear. I have to consider what my peers will say and whether or not my teachers will send me to the dean for a dress code violation. Then I still need approval from my mom. It just takes forever. For these and so many more reasons, I'd actually rather have a uniform. Therefore, I am in favor of a school-wide uniform policy.

Body Paragraphs

First of all, I believe that most of us students would be happier if we had uniforms. Getting our minds off fashion and onto our education would greatly improve our classroom behavior (and grades). One effect of having a school-wide uniform policy is that no longer will we students have to be afraid that we aren't wearing designer name brands. I know my older sister wore a blue-light special red shirt and was made fun of all year. The girls in her class even called her "blue-light special" all year long. It wasn't her fault that our mom couldn't afford a name brand shirt with a recognizable logo on the front. Overall, uniforms would make all of us students feel equal with our peers, and of course, happier.

In addition to happier students, I believe the school would have happier teachers. Spending less time on dress code violations would allow teachers to have more time for teaching. Also, the students wouldn't be distracted so much by the latest fashion, so they would be able to pay attention to the teachers better. What teacher wouldn't like that? Besides just having the students' attention and being able to actually teach, the teachers would also have less harassment in the classroom. Students would no longer be able to wear designer name brands if a uniform policy is in effect. Then students would no longer be teased for what they wear. Basically, teachers would be happier with more time to teach and with students who pay attention to the lesson.

Finally, I know for a fact many of the parents would be happier if the students had uniforms. My mom likes to talk on the phone to a lot of other moms, voicing her opinion on this matter. She said that every mom she talked to is in favor of school-wide uniforms. My mom said that with uniforms, she would have more money to spend on the family, including me! I guess we could go to the movies more, and do things we can't do now because of the cost of clothes. In addition to saving money, she and the other mothers know that students face a lot of stress when we go to school. They know that we worry if we are going to be made fun of because of our outfits. My mom was really upset when my sister came home with her new nickname. With a school-wide uniform policy, though, even our moms (and dads, too) would be happier.

Conclusion

Mr. Principal, when you have your PTA meeting, I can guarantee you that more than half of the moms will cheer and clap in support of a school-wide uniform policy. But remember, we students and teachers would be happier, too. This policy will bring you a better, safer school. I urge you to put the school-wide uniform policy into effect immediately.

PRACTICE WRITING THE PERSUASIVE ESSAY

Now, you can take what you have learned about writing persuasive essays and put it into practice. Go through all the steps outlined in this chapter before you begin writing the essay. Do not forget to write down the time you begin reading the prompt and also record the time you finish writing your essay. Try to budget your time wisely for each of the four steps when writing your essay. Recording the time you spend on your essay will provide a guideline for how long it will take you on the big day.

Persuasive Prompt Practice

Writing Situation: *A new high school will be built in your neighborhood. The new principal is holding a contest to find a mascot for the new school.*

Directions for Writing: Choose a mascot that you would like to have at your new school. Now persuade the new principal in writing to choose your mascot.

Time: _____

Planning Page (This page will *not* be scored. Any information you write in this section will not be considered.)

Begin your essay here:

_____

_____

_____

_____

_____

_____

_____

_____

_____

_____

_____

_____

_____

_____

_____

_____

_____

_____

_____

ADDITIONAL ESSAY PROMPTS

Use the essay prompts below as additional practice before the FCAT Writing+ Test.

1. Expository

   Writing Situation: *Everyone has a hero, someone they admire or look up to.*

   Directions for Writing: *Before you begin writing, think about who your hero is and why. Now explain why this person is your hero.*

2. Persuasive

   Writing Situation: *The principal of your school has decided to review the policy of chewing gum in school. At this time, students are not allowed to chew gum in school at all.*

   Directions for Writing: *Before you begin writing, decide if you would like to change the policy or if you would like it to remain the same. Now convince your principal in writing tto support your point of view about chewing gum.*

3. Expository

   Writing Situation: *Everyone has jobs or chores.*

   Directions for Writing: *Before you begin writing, think about why you do one of your jobs or chores. Now explain why you do this job or chore.*

4. Persuasive

   Writing Situation: *The principal of your school has been asked to discuss with a group of parents how TV watching affects students' grades.*

   Directions for Writing: *Think about the effect watching TV has on your grades and your friends' grades. Now write to convince your parents to accept your point of view and to share it with the principal.*

5. Expository

Writing Situation: *The U.S. Postal Service has honored many individuals by placing their portraits on postage stamps. Whom would you nominate to be honored with a postage stamp?*

Directions for Writing: *Before you begin to write, think about why this person or character should have his or her own stamp. Now write an essay telling the reader whom you would choose and explain why that person should be honored with a postage stamp. Support your ideas with examples and details.*

6. Persuasive

Writing Situation: *A growing problem in your school is the disruption caused by cell phones and pagers used by students. The Board of Education wants to develop a policy regulating or banning electronic devices and is asking students for input.*

Directions for Writing: *Before you begin to write, think about the possible solutions for developing a policy regulating or banning electronic devices. Now write a letter to the Board of Education convincing them to develop the policy or policies you suggest.*

7. Expository

Writing Situation: *Everyone has a favorite type of music.*

Directions for Writing: *Before you begin to write, think about your favorite kind of music and why you like it. Now explain in an essay why this type of music has become your favorite.*

8. Persuasive

Writing Situation: *A local radio station is planning to partner with one middle school to promote education to the community. Students' actual voices will be recorded for short radio spots.*

Directions for Writing: *Before you begin to write, think about the reasons why your school and your voice should be chosen. Now write an essay persuading the manager of the local radio station to partner with your school and to use your voice on the radio.*

9. Expository

Writing Situation: *Most people have a favorite music group or singer.*

Directions for Writing: *Before you begin to write, think about a music group or singer you particularly like. Now explain in writing why this music group or singer is your favorite.*

10. Persuasive

Writing Situation: *The Florida Legislature is discussing the possibility of removing extracurricular activities from the regular school day so that more time is spent on academic areas (language arts, reading, social studies, science, math).*

Directions for Writing: *Before you begin to write, think about the effects of removing extracurricular activities from the regular school day. Now persuade the adult reader of your paper to agree with your view on whether to remove extracurricular activities from the regular school day.*

11. Persuasive

Writing Situation: *Each year many tourists visit Florida in the summer. The Florida Department of Tourism wants to create a commercial drawing tourists to Florida from all over the country.*

Directions for Writing: *Before you begin to write, think about the reasons that make Florida a great vacation spot in the summer. Now write a commercial that persuades tourists from other states to choose Florida as their vacation spot this summer.*

12. Expository

Writing Situation: *Most students think of one day or event as their favorite one.*

Directions for Writing: *Before you begin to write, think about your favorite day or event. Now explain in writing the reasons it is your favorite.*

TIPS FOR PARENTS

■ Spend time talking about your family as you go through photo albums. This will give your child many stories from which to draw during the test if he or she is given an expository topic about a person or event.

■ Watch the evening news and read articles from the newspaper together. This will keep your child aware of current events that may be mentioned in a persuasive topic. Engage in discussions and debates about current events to help your child evaluate situations. It is important to note, however, that your child will be not be given a topic he or she has not heard anything about.

■ Ask your child about issues he or she may be facing at school. These are very commonly used as writing prompts, such as the school dress code and cafeteria food. Explore both the pros and the cons, as this will help your child understand both sides of an argument.

■ Have your child go to bed on time (early if possible) the night before the test. Then, make sure your child eats a healthy breakfast the morning of the test. Surprisingly, these two simple actions can actually boost your child's energy and thinking ability the day of the test.

- Discuss the topics mentioned in the additional essay prompts before this section.
- Give positive reinforcement for the effort your child is making and his or her progress.

TIPS FOR TEACHERS

- Encourage students to spend time talking with their families about family members and significant events.
- Require essays as homework assignments all year long, not just the month before the test.
- Explain that it is better to use a more challenging word rather than a simple word, even if the student is not sure of the spelling; always include vocabulary lessons when reading literature, as these are a great source of higher-level words for students.
- Introduce students to alternate words for overused verbs, as well as synonyms for many adjectives (for example, encourage students to replace forms of the verb "to be" with more active verbs and teach students to use a better vocabulary word like "scarlet" in place of "red").
- Provide timed writing exercises throughout the year so that students learn how to budget their time for this particular test.
- Teach students how to use effective transitions within paragraphs as well as between paragraphs.
- Encourage open discussions or debates in class about relevant social topics. Explore both sides of issues thoroughly so that students understand the pros and cons of arguments.
- Evaluate students' writing for focus, organization, support, and conventions throughout the year so that they are familiar with how important these four elements are to their finished writing.
- Provide student practice in scoring essays, both their own and their peers'.

■ Allow students to practice evaluating each other's work; this also helps them evaluate their own writing style.

■ Provide essay prompts written in FCAT format ("Writing Situation" and "Directions for Writing") that are interesting. Get them excited about writing so that, regardless of the topic, they are ready to write the day of the test.

■ Use the additional essay prompts just before this section as practice exercises for your students.

SUGGESTED ANSWERS

Hook Practice

The following sentences are examples of how you can use effective hooks in your writing. There are other ways of writing the sentences, though.

1. When I smell garlic bread, I know my mom has made my favorite Italian meal of spaghetti and homemade meatballs.
2. Many teenagers would be exposed to harmful lyrics if CDs did not have parental warnings.
3. What is ruining Florida's beaches?
4. Without electives, school would be one long math class!
5. Our principal announced, "This year's teacher of the year is Mrs. Jones!"

Figurative Language Practice

The following sentences are examples of how you can use figurative language in your writing. There are other ways of writing the sentences, though.

Metaphors

1. Your cat is a pig!
2. My uncle is a lion because he roars whenever we track mud through the house.
3. My school is a prison because we have so many strict rules.
4. Breakfast on Sundays is pure heaven.
5. The grass in my front yard is a jungle.

Similes

1. John's dog smells like a skunk.
2. My room looks like a pigsty.
3. My brother's car is as fast as a racecar.
4. The street near the library looks like a dump.
5. The book I have to read for English is as big as a house.

Personification

1. The garage door burst open.
2. The kitten loudly protested when I left for school.
3. The bathroom light winked.
4. My hat sits on my head.
5. The airplane ran down the runway and jumped into the sky.

Imagery

1. I love to watch the foamy, white waves at the beach.
2. I love to kick the soccer ball so hard that my foot stings.
3. My mom's creamy mashed potatoes taste great with her thick, rich gravy.
4. The trumpets' horns during band practice make my ears ring.
5. Thanksgiving dinner smells like a mixture of pumpkin pie, juicy baked turkey, and sweet potatoes.

Vocabulary Practice

The following sentences are examples of how you can use the words from the vocabulary list in your writing. There are other ways of writing the sentences, though.

1. The cafeteria was desolate after lunch.
2. My grandmother's chronic disease affected her until she died.
3. Many people tell me that I am amiable.
4. Even though my teacher is very intelligent, she can still be fallible about current trends!
5. I want to dissuade my principal from banning cell phones at school.

Proofreading and Editing Practice

1. Remember to look at your notes before you take the test. The wrong word was used in this sentence. "You're" means "you are," but the possessive pronoun "your" was intended to modify "notes."
2. When I heard Dad call my name, I knew I had been caught. *"Dad" must be capitalized in this sentence because it is used as a name, not just as a description of who the person is.*
3. Every time I want to walk my dog, the rain starts to pour. *A comma is needed after "dog" to indicate the end of an introductory phrase.*
4. There are many people in the world who do not understand the meaning of peace. *"There" is the correct spelling for this sentence. "Their" means "belonging to them."*
5. When will you be available to study with me for the big test? *The correct punctuation for this sentence is a question mark indicating that a question has been asked.*
6. Mom went to the grocery store, but she forgot her checkbook. *This sentence requires a comma after "store" to indicate a compound sentence that has*

two independent clauses joined by a conjunction.

7. I have a lot of homework tonight. *The word "a lot" is two words, not one.*

8. In an outline, use Roman numerals to indicate the major headings. *"Roman" is a proper adjective that must be capitalized.*

9. Weren't you in my first-period class, too? *An apostrophe is needed to show that "were not" has been contracted.*

10. Have you read the book <u>Animal Farm</u>? <u>*Animal Farm*</u> *is the name of a book and must be capitalized.*

11. *One way to rewrite*: One quality about my teacher that I like is that she takes the time to listen to my questions. *The word "thing" has been replaced with a more specific noun, "quality."*

12. *One way to rewrite*: Tommy, my classmate excels in every sport he plays. *Replace the verb "is" with "excels" and make "everything" a more specific noun.*

13. *One way to rewrite*: Sally plays in the school band and sings in the choir, too. *Sometimes it is better to combine two short sentences into one to avoid repetition. Use an appropriate conjunction and correct punctuation when combining sentences, though.*

14. *One way to rewrite*: How many books are in your backpack? *The word "stuff" is not specific. Replace it with a more specific noun like "books" and change the verb to "are."*

15. *One way to rewrite*: Jamal works hard. *Avoid using forms of the verb "to be" in sentences. Replace it with an active verb like "works."*

16. *One way to rewrite*: My sister does not tell the truth. *Replace the verb "is" with a more active verb like "tell."*

17. *One way to rewrite*: I love summer for many reasons. *Avoid beginning a sentence with "there are." Instead, just begin the sentence.*

18. *One way to rewrite*: All the books and papers in my locker started to smell because I left my lunch in there over the weekend. *It's much more specific to tell what "everything" is in this sentence. Describing the items using "all the books and papers" gives a much more clear picture.*

19. *One way to rewrite*: After school, I will return your video game. *Sometimes taking a phrase from the end of a sentence and placing it at the beginning makes the sentence more interesting. Here, "after school" was moved to the beginning to change the sentence structure.*

20. *One way to rewrite*: My friend John plays soccer better than the other players on the team. *Replace the verb "is" with a more active verb like "plays."*

Chapter 4

Taking the FCAT Writing+ Test (Multiple Choice)

The FCAT Writing+ Test is made up of one essay and 45 to 50 multiple-choice questions. In the previous chapter, you were prepared for the essay portion. This chapter will guide you through all the basics of the multiple-choice section.

Each answer is worth 1 point, so make sure you answer all the questions by bubbling in an answer choice. You will not be asked to write anything in this section of the Writing+ Test; rather you will always be given either three or four choices.

You will be allowed two 40-minute sessions for this test. Be sure to read each passage or writing sample before answering the questions about it. Then go through the questions and choose the best answer. If you are unsure of an answer, make your best guess, mark the question, and come back to it at the end.

Throughout this chapter, you will study how to read the grammar questions and writing samples. Then you will practice choosing the correct answer. Finally, you will be given a short practice test that will help you prepare for the FCAT Writing+ Test (Multiple Choice). After you finish the practice materials, score your answers and determine which areas you should study.

TYPES OF GRAMMAR SELECTIONS

Tip: The FCAT Writing+ Test (Multiple Choice) measures your skills in focus, organization, support, and conventions.

The FCAT Writing+ Test (Multiple Choice) was added to the FCAT in order to assess your knowledge of focus, organization, support, and conventions. These areas are also measured in the FCAT Writing+ Test (Essay), but the evaluators are not able to specifically measure all types of skills in just one essay. That's why this section was created.

There are two types of selections on the FCAT Writing+ Test that measure your knowledge of focus, organization, and support:

- prewriting, including outlines and webs
- drafting, including student-written texts

There are two types of selections on the FCAT Writing+ Test that measure your knowledge of basic language conventions:

- short passages, mostly informative texts, in which you choose the correct spelling or usage
- single sentences in which you choose correct spelling, capitalization, usage, punctuation, or sentence structure

CHOOSING THE CORRECT ANSWER (MULTIPLE-CHOICE QUESTIONS)

Tip: Trust your first instinct! Your first guess is probably the right answer.

If you believe you know the answer immediately, you probably do. Your first instinct should be trusted when answering multiple-choice questions. If you do not have a strong feeling for the answer, though, first eliminate every choice that you know is not correct. Then you will not be looking at so many choices. Another basic strategy to help you when answering multiple-choice questions is to cover up the answers and try to answer the question without looking at the choices. Then uncover the choices and see if your answer is listed. You will have a great chance for success with this method.

Also, refer to the text. The answer may not be stated word for word in an answer choice, so take your time to reread parts of the passage. Sometimes the choices have been reworded to test your comprehension and vocabulary skills. Other times, the choices are testing your higher-level thinking skills such as how well you can apply the information to a new situation or how well you evaluate the text.

WRITING REVIEW: FOCUS, ORGANIZATION, SUPPORT

You will be given various writing samples in different stages of the writing process, including outlines or webs, and student drafts. These passages will test your knowledge and skills in three main areas: focus, organization, and support. Each question in this section has four answer choices, but no extended responses or short responses are required.

Outline/Web Practice

Seth made the outline below to organize his thoughts before the school elections. Some of the details under the subtopics have not been listed yet. Read the writing plan and answer questions 1 through 6. (The questions have been labeled with the skill being tested.)

<u>My Outline</u>

   I.   Why I'm the best candidate for class president
  II. Dependable
 III. Involved
      A.
      B.
      C.
 IV. Experience
      A.
      B.
      C.
  V. Vote for me!

Support Question

1. Which details should be listed under the subtopic "involved"?
   A. no tardies, less than 5 absences per year, excellent attendance in clubs
   B. worked with last year's president, good relationship with teachers
   C. member of several clubs, play sports, understand students' needs
   D. not a member of band, played on soccer team in grade school

Focus Question

2. The subtopics of this formal outline indicate that the topic would be
   F. perfect for a research paper
   G. too broad for an essay
   H. perfect for a short speech
   I. too detailed for an editorial

Support Question

3. Under which subtopic should details about attendance be placed?
   A. why I'm the best candidate for class president
   B. dependable
   C. involved
   D. experience as treasurer

Student Draft Practice

The essay below is a first draft that Jackson wrote for his teacher. The essay contains errors. Read the essay and answer the following questions. (The questions have been labeled with the skill being tested.)

[1] Who likes to be eaten up by mosquitoes? [2] I know I don't. [3] But I believe there are several ways to avoid being bug food during the summer.

[4] This year, I'm ready to battle those little annoyances with my very own homemade bug repellant. [5] For last year's science project, I researched the best ingredients in herbal bug sprays and tested all sorts of herbs and oils. [6] Only one plant worked the best lemon grass stalks rubbed directly on the skin. [7] To my amazement, this kept me free from mosquito bites. [8] Apparently, the oil in the plant is even stronger than citronella.

[9] My family has inspected our yard for any standing water. [10] If you have anything that collects rainwater without draining, either get rid of it or dump it out regularly. [11] Mosquitoes love to breed in standing water, so if you get rid of it in your yard, you will definitely have less bug bites!

[12] Sometimes local government officials are nice to talk to. [13] The last method of attack we have planned is that our city council voted to increase the amount of times that mosquito trucks patrol the neighborhoods, releasing the toxic chemicals to the little pests. [14] My classmates and I worked hard to get enough signatures to have the issue put on a ballot earlier this year.

[15] This year, I expect to win the battle against the mosquito. [16] I guess I'll let you know next year how all of these methods worked.

Support Question

1. Which sentence should be deleted because it presents a detail that is unimportant to the essay?
   A. the first sentence of paragraph 2
   B. the last sentence of paragraph 2
   C. the first sentence of paragraph 4
   D. the last sentence of paragraph 4

Support Question

2. Read the sentence below.

   To our satisfaction, the board agreed with us and decided to spend more money on this needed expense.

   To which paragraph should this sentence be added in Jackson's essay?
   F. paragraph 1
   G. paragraph 2
   H. paragraph 3
   I. paragraph 4

Organization Question

3. Which transition should be added to the beginning of paragraph 3 to show the connection between ideas in the essay?
   A. When summer ends,
   B. After we go outside,
   C. The last method of defense against mosquitoes,
   D. In addition to my new bug repellent,

Focus Question

4. Which sentence below does NOT support any of the main points of the story?
   F. Mosquitoes are annoying little pests.
   G. My family and I work together to reduce our risk of exposure to mosquitoes.
   H. My favorite plant to grow is lemon grass.
   I. I enjoyed finding ways of protecting myself against mosquitoes and learned a lot in the process.

Organization Question

5. Where should the following sentence be added to the essay?

   Every year, my mom tries to find an effective bug repellant, but so far we've had no luck.

   A. after sentence 1
   B. before sentence 4
   C. after sentence 8
   D. before sentence 12

GRAMMAR REVIEW: CONVENTIONS

In this section of the FCAT, you will be given two different types of selections: short informational texts and single sentences.

These passages test your knowledge and skills in the area of conventions, specifically sentence structure, spelling, usage, capitalization, and punctuation. Each question in this section has only three answer choices, but there are no extended responses or short responses.

Let's quickly review each of these five areas of conventions, touching on the main skills tested on the FCAT. After we've reviewed and practiced each grammar skill, you will be given a shorter version of the FCAT Writing+ Test (Multiple Choice).

Capitalization

IMPORTANT RULES TO REMEMBER

Always capitalize the following.

■ proper nouns: proper names, holidays and calendar items, historical events and periods, nationalities, races, religions, brand names of business products, any other particular places, things, or events.

   Example:
   We will have a school holiday on **Memorial Day**.
   My mom replaced the **Kleenex** box in the bathroom.

■ proper pronouns

Example:

"Wow!" **I** exclaimed.

■ proper adjectives

Example:

My teacher taught us how to use **Roman** numerals in a formal outline.

■ the first word in a sentence

Example:

The bread was fresh from the oven.

■ the first word in a quotation

Example:

When the cat ran out the door, my brother screamed, "**Catch** him!"

■ titles

Example:

Robert Frost's poem "**Stopping by Woods**" is my favorite one to read.

Never capitalize the following.

■ names of school subjects (except languages and courses that have a number following the name)

Capitalization Practice

Circle the words that should be capitalized.

1. we will finish studying english literature this semester.
2. jeb bush is the governor of florida.
3. the month of june is my favorite for surfing.
4. washington middle school has approximately 1,000 students.
5. i just finished reading the most recent harry potter book.

Punctuation

IMPORTANT RULES TO REMEMBER

Always use the following end marks.

- ■ a period to indicate a declarative sentence
- ■ an exclamation mark to indicate an exclamation
- ■ a question mark to indicate a question

Examples:
The school bell rang loudly. (*period*)
I just can't believe it! (*exclamation point*)
When will supper be ready? (*question mark*)

In sentences and/or phrases, use

- ■ a colon to indicate a list will follow.

Example:
The following will be on our holiday menu: turkey, stuffing, mashed potatoes, corn, gravy, and bread.

- ■ a semicolon to indicate separation between the parts of a compound sentence if they are not joined by a conjunction.

Example:
Baseball is my favorite sport; I love to pass the time swinging the bat for practice.

- ■ quotes to indicate
  a direct quote
  titles of short texts (like songs, short stories, and poems)

Examples:
Carlos said, "Wait for me, Jimmy."
"The Star Spangled Banner" brings tears to my eyes.

■ commas to separate
items in a list
two or more adjectives before a noun
dates and addresses

Examples:
My brother's favorite animals at the zoo are the snakes, lizards, and exotic frogs.
The excited, eager student awaited his test results.
America officially gained its independence on July 4, 1777.

Use the following punctuation with words.

■ an apostrophe to indicate
possession
a contraction

Examples:
The **tree's** leaves are starting to fall.
Don't forget to take out the trash.

■ underlining or italics to indicate the title of a long text (books, plays, and so on)

Example:
My school's drama team is performing <u>**The Diary of Anne Frank**</u> this year.

OR

My school's drama team is performing *The Diary of Anne Frank* this year.

Punctuation Practice

Insert the correct punctuation in each sentence.

1. My teachers attitude was great when she told us we scored well on this years FCAT test
2. Have you learned how to take compliments well
3. I began practicing the following skills in order to be a better player dribbling running shooting
4. Help

5. Ruth told me Stop acting so grown up youre only thirteen
6. Molly took her own sweet time going to class however I rushed
7. Do you live in Tallahasse Florida
8. William Shakespeare wrote Romeo and Juliet
9. Our national anthem is The Star Spangled Banner
10. Because my grades have improved I will pass the course

Usage

IMPORTANT RULES TO REMEMBER

In every piece of writing, keep agreement between

■ subject and verb

Examples:
My **relatives are** difficult to be around. (plural noun + plural verb)
Each of my test scores **was** telling the story that I didn't study.

■ pronoun and antecedent

Example:
The **team** won **its** first state championship.
Every **one** of my classmates studied for **his** final exams.

OR

Every **one** of my classmates studied for **his or her** final exams.

Usage Practice

Circle the correct word in parentheses that fits the blank in the sentence.

1. Everybody should know _____ address. (his/their)
2. One of the lights on my porch ___ not work. (does/do)

3. He borrowed my equipment and didn't return
_____. (them/it)

4. I believe you _____ too much for your shoes.
(pay/pays)

5. Flocks of birds _____ south each year in the fall.
(fly/flies)

Sentence Structure

IMPORTANT RULES TO REMEMBER

There are three main types of sentences:

- A simple sentence is one independent clause (one
  subject and one verb).

  Example:
  The **bird flew** around his cage. (subject + verb)

- A compound sentence contains two or more independent clauses.

  Example:
  The **bird flew** around his cage, **but he rested** after
  five minutes. (subject + verb + subject + verb)

- A complex sentence has one independent clause and
  at least one subordinate clause (a phrase that cannot
  stand on its own).

  Example:
  The **bird rested** because he was tired. (subject + verb
  + adverb clause)

Sentence Structure Practice

Label each sentence properly with *simple, compound,* or
complex.

1. My favorite hobbies are reading and playing softball.

2. When I visited my aunt last summer, I learned how
to take care of her two very independent cats.

3. My little brother likes to play in the mud, and he always comes inside messy.
4. Many people like to travel during summer vacation.
5. Florida's beaches are like a playground for many people, and others find the sandy places to be a source of relaxation.

Spelling

IMPORTANT RULES TO REMEMBER

Spell words correctly when adding

- prefixes (the word stays the same when adding a prefix).

  Examples:
  il + legible = illegible
  mis + understand = misunderstand

- suffixes (sometimes the spelling changes when adding a suffix).

  Examples:
  sudden + *ly* = suddenly
  care + *less* = careless

Form plurals of nouns by

- adding *s* to most regular nouns.
- adding *es* if the noun ends in *s, x, z, ch,* or *sh*.
- changing the *y* to *i* and adding *es*.

  Examples:
  table + *s* = tables
  stitch + *es* = stitches
  lady + *es* = ladies

Know the basic spelling rules:

- *i* before *e* except after *c* or if it sounds like *a,* as in "neighbor" and "weigh" (exception: "weird").

Study the following list of commonly misspelled and/or confused words:

- accept/except
- advice/advise
- affect/effect
- allowed/aloud
- all right/alright
- a lot/allot
- already/all ready
- beautiful
- because
- first/second/and so on
- flour/flower
- for/four/fore
- herd/heard
- its/it's
- license
- new/knew
- no/know
- principal/principle
- probably
- received
- see/sea
- surprise
- than/then
- their/there/they're
- threw/through
- too/two/to
- until
- week/weak
- whether/weather
- where/wear
- who's/whose
- witch/which
- your/you're

Spelling Practice

Circle the incorrectly spelled words and write in the correct spelling.

1. We forgot to bring matchs for our campfire.
2. Many European countries except the Euro as payment.
3. In order too understand my teacher better, I moved closer to the front of the class.
4. My favorite teacher is my sceince teacher because he makes learning fun.
5. All of the familys in my subdivision have complained about my dad's rusty old car in the front yard.
6. We will probly move to another city when our house sells.
7. The sunsets at the beach are beutiful.
8. Their are many causes of pollution in the river.
9. Our new nieghbors brought us a cake when we moved in to our new house.
10. When all of my brothers and sisters are at practice, the house is so pieceful.

Article Practice

Hurricanes and Tornadoes

[1] Hurricanes and (1) _____ are both severe weather events, but they are different in many ways.

[2] A hurricane gives people at least a day's warning, but a tornado only (2) _____ a few minutes' warning. [3] Although (3) _____ are getting better at predicting severe (4) _____ _____ are still not 100% accurate.

[4] Tornadoes and hurricanes both cause a lot of damage. [5] A tornado's damage is usually over a smaller area than a (5) _____ damage. [6] Some hurricanes have even caused damage in many cities affecting hundreds of thousands of people. [7] Tornadoes usually affect less than a thousand.

Spelling

1. Which answer should go in blank 1?
    A. tornados
    B. tornadoes
    C. tornado's

Usage

2. Which answer should go in blank 2?
    F. gives
    G. give
    H. gave

Capitalization

3. Which answer should go in blank 3?
    A. scientists'
    B. Scientists
    C. scientists

Sentence Structure

4. Which answer should go in blank 4?
    F. weather, they
    G. weather. They
    H. weather: they

Punctuation

5. Which answer should go in blank 5?
    A. hurricanes'
    B. hurricane's
    C. hurricanes

Stand-Alone Items Practice
Spelling

1. My teacher has _____ of quirks about her.
    A. a lot
    B. allot
    C. alot

Usage

2. Blue jeans have become fashionable all over the world; the American originators _____ still wear more jeans than anyone else.
    F. however
    G. however,
    H. however,

Capitalization

3. In which sentence below is all the capitalization correct?
    A. My favorite subjects in school are Spanish and Mathematics.
    B. My favorite subjects in school are spanish and mathematics.
    C. My favorite subjects in school are Spanish and mathematics.

Sentence Structure

4. I did not buy the _____ borrowed it instead.
    F. book. i
    G. book I
    H. book; I

Punctuation

5. When _____ your turn to read, speak clearly.
    A. its
    B. it's
    C. its'

SAMPLE TEST: FCAT WRITING+ (MULTIPLE CHOICE)

This is not a complete practice test—two complete tests can be found at the end of this book.

Elizabeth made the writing plan below to organize ideas for a paper she is writing. Read the writing plan and answer questions 1 through 3.

How to Bake the Perfect Batch of Cookies

I.   Perfect batch of cookies
II. Preparation
    A. Ingredients
    B. Utensils
III. Mixing
IV. Baking
V.   Serving

1. Under which subtopic should details about a bowl, a mixer, and cookie sheets be placed?
   A. Utensils
   B. Mixing
   C. Serving
   D. none of the above

2. Based on the writing plan, what kind of paper is Elizabeth planning to write?
   F. a paper that explains the characteristics of a good cook
   G. a paper that compares two different types of cookies
   H. a paper that describes the steps to baking good cookies
   I. a paper that persuades the reader to bake cookies from scratch

3. Which detail below supports the subtopic "Ingredients"?
   A. flour
   B. eggs
   C. sugar
   D. all of the above

The essay below is a first draft that Dawn wrote for her teacher. The essay contains errors. Read the essay and answer questions 4 through 8.

[1] One summer, my parents surprised me with a trip to a 4H summer camp. [2] Ever since I could remember, I had always wanted to go away for a few weeks to be with our kids my age. [3] But the biggest surprise was that this particular 4H camp also had horses! [4] I must have five posters of horses in my room.

[5] From the first day of camp when we were introduced to the horse we would be taking care of for the next two weeks, I fell in love. [6] His name was Trotsie, which was very appropreate. [7] He loved to trot around on the trails with me and the other kids on their horses.

[8] Learning to care for horses taught me a lot of responsibility that summer. [9] I had to learned how to feed Trotsie, clean his stall, and brush his beautiful brown coat. [10] At first, I didn't want to clean out the stall because it smelled so bad, but after awhile, it was worth it to be able to ride him every day.

[11] I sure do wish I could have my own horse someday. [12] But living in a two bedroom apartment on the second floor wouldn't accommodate that type of pet!

4. Which sentence contains a spelling error?
   F. sentence 3
   G. sentence 6
   H. sentence 9
   I. sentence 12

5. Which sentence should be deleted from the first paragraph to maintain focus?
   A. the first one
   B. the second
   C. the last one
   D. none; the paragraph is focused

6. Which sentence should be deleted because it presents a detail that is unrelated to the main points of the essay?
   F. sentence 2
   G. sentence 5
   H. sentence 11
   I. sentence 12

7. Dawn wants to add the sentence below to her article:

   I never could image that I would love an animal so much and so quickly.

   Where should this sentence be added to keep the details in the correct order?
   A. to the beginning of paragraph 2
   B. to the beginning of paragraph 3
   C. to the end of paragraph 2
   D. to the beginning of paragraph 4

8. Which sentence below should Dawn add to conclude her essay with a summary?
   F. My experience at 4H camp has grown my love for horses.
   G. I'll never want to go back to school again.
   H. My parents are the best parents ever.
   I. Dogs are also great pets.

Read the following article on pollution in Florida and answer questions 9 through 12.

Pollution on Florida's Beaches

[1] Pollution is ruining some of Florida's beaches. [2] Careless beachgoers are taking away the beauty of what makes Florida so (9) _____ beautiful and relaxing beaches. [3] Many cities are trying to get the message out that trashing Florida's beaches is not acceptable.

[4] Everyone knows that picking up after a visit to the beach is important. [5] Many public beaches have large trash bins conveniently placed. [6] Some groups and organizations even volunteer their time on a weekend to pick up (10) _____ local beach.

[7] Also, some cities in Florida have created commercials asking residents to help keep the beaches clean. [8] Cleverly written, these television spots encourage all (11) _____ to help keep the beaches clean.

[9] With help from everyone, (12) _____ will be enjoyed for many years to come by the people who visit them every day.

Choose the word or words that correctly complete the questions.

9. Which answer should go in blank 9?
   A. special: it's
   B. special; it's
   C. special. It's

10. Which answer should go in blank 10?
   F. they're
   G. their
   H. there

11. Which answer should go in blank 11?
    A. beachgoers, residents, and tourists alike,
    B. beachgoers, residents, and tourists, alike
    C. beachgoers, residents, and tourists alike

12. Which answer should go in blank 12?
    F. Floridas beaches
    G. Florida's beach's
    H. Florida's beaches

Answer questions 13 through 20.

13. In which sentence below are all the grammar and usage correct?
    A. Her and I have the same algebra teacher.
    B. She and I have the same algebra teacher.
    C. Her and me have the same algebra teacher.

14. In which sentence below is the capitalization correct?
    F. The St. Johns River runs through the state of Florida.
    G. The St. Johns River runs through the State of Florida.
    H. The St. Johns river runs through the state of Florida.

15. In which sentence below is all the sentence structure correct?
    A. She reads French and can speak it a little.
    B. She reads French and she can speak it a little.
    C. She reads French, and can speak it a little.

16. In which sentence below is all the punctuation correct?
    F. The woman who is a doctor cares for her invalid father.
    G. The woman, who is a doctor, cares for her invalid father.
    H. The woman who is a doctor, cares for her invalid father.

17. In which sentence below are all the grammar and usage correct?
   A. Before everyone had a chance to study her notes, the teacher sprung a pop quiz on the class.
   B. Before everyone had a chance to study their notes, the teacher sprung a pop quiz on the class.
   C. Before everyone had a chance to study his notes, the teacher sprung a pop quiz on the class.

18. In which sentence below is all the spelling correct?
   F. The dog licked its wounds after fighting with the neighborhood cat.
   G. The dog licked it's wounds after fighting with the neighborhood cat.
   H. The dog licked its' wounds after fighting with the neighborhood cat.

19. In which sentence below is all the grammar and usage correct?
   A. A bunch of grapes cost less than a bushel of apples.
   B. A bunch of grapes cost less then a bushel of apples.
   C. A bunch of grapes costs less than a bushel of apples.

20. In which sentence below is all the spelling correct?
   F. If the weather permits, then our playoff game will be held this afternoon.
   G. If the whether permits, than our playoff game will be held this afternoon.
   H. If the weather permits, than our playoff game will be held this afternoon.

TIPS FOR PARENTS

- Encourage your child to read; that's where he or she will learn good grammar.
- Many commercials use poor grammar in their advertising. Watch television together and try to find the grammatical mistakes (for example, McDonald's slogan "i'm lovin' it").
- Internet lingo is also full of poor grammar. Have your child make a list of all the incorrect grammar used in email or instant messaging (for example, LUV, LOL).
- Use correct grammar yourself. Modeling good grammar is the best teacher for your child.

TIPS FOR TEACHERS

- Use daily language activities to strengthen students' basic grammar skills.
- Use peer editing in your classroom. The more your students look at other students' work and are asked to evaluate them, the better they will become at evaluating their own work.
- Provide plenty of practice in all stages of writing— prewriting, drafting, editing, revising. Students with a lot of practice in all stages of the writing process are better able to identify mistakes.
- Require a lot of reading from your students.
- Divide the class into five groups. Assign each group one of the sections of conventions to study, and prepare a lesson to teach to the rest of the class. Each group should also provide practice activities and an evaluation. This will strengthen skills beyond simple grammar practice in at least one area.
- Spend time reviewing irregular forms of nouns and verbs, as these forms were not covered in this chapter.

ANSWERS

Writing Review: Focus, Organization, Support
Outline/Web Practice

1. The correct answer is C (member of several clubs, play sports, understand students' needs).
2. The correct answer is H (perfect for a short speech).
3. The correct answer is B (dependable).

Student Draft Practice

1. The correct answer is C (first sentence of paragraph 4).
2. The correct answer is I (four).
3. The correct answer is D (In addition to my new bug repellent).
4. The correct answer is H (My favorite plant to grow is lemon grass).
5. The correct answer is B (before sentence 4).

Grammar Review: Conventions
Capitalization Practice

1. The word(s) that should have been capitalized include: we, english.
2. The word(s) that should have been capitalized include: jeb, bush, florida.
3. The word(s) that should have been capitalized include: the, june.
4. The word(s) that should have been capitalized include: washington middle school.
5. The word(s) that should have been capitalized include: i, harry potter.

Punctuation Practice

1. The correct answer is: My teacher's attitude was great when she told us we scored well on this years FCAT test.
2. The correct answer is: Have you learned how to take compliments well?
3. The correct answer is: I began practicing the following skills in order to be a better player: dribbling, running, shooting.
4. The correct answer is: Help!
5. The correct answer is: Ruth told me, "Stop acting so grown up. You're only thirteen." (An exclamation point would also be acceptable for one of the two periods.)
6. The correct answer is: Molly took her own, sweet time going to class; however, I rushed.
7. The correct answer is: Do you live in Tallahasse, Florida?
8. The correct answer is: William Shakespeare wrote <u>Romeo and Juliet</u>.
9. The correct answer is: Our national anthem is "The Star-Spangled Banner."
10. The correct answer is: Because my grades have improved, I will pass the course.

Usage Practice

1. The correct answer is *his* because it agrees with the noun "everybody."
2. The correct answer is *do* because it agrees with the subject "One."
3. The correct answer is *it* because it agrees with the noun "equipment."
4. The correct answer is *pay* because it agrees with the subject "you."
5. The correct answer is *fly* because it agrees with the subject "Flocks."

Sentence Structure Practice

1. The correct answer is *simple.*
2. The correct answer is *complex.*
3. The correct answer is *compound.*
4. The correct answer is *simple.*
5. The correct answer is *compound.*

Spelling Practice

1. The correct answer is *matches.*
2. The correct answer is *accept.*
3. The correct answer is *to.*
4. The correct answer is *science.*
5. The correct answer is *families.*
6. The correct answer is *probably.*
7. The correct answer is *beautiful.*
8. The correct answer is *There.*
9. The correct answer is *neighbor.*
10. The correct answer is *peaceful.*

Article Practice

1. The correct answer is B (tornadoes).
2. The correct answer is F (gives).
3. The correct answer is C (scientists).
4. The correct answer is F (weather, they).
5. The correct answer is B (hurricane's).

Stand-Alone Practice

1. The correct answer is A (a lot).
2. The correct answer is H (however,).
3. The correct answer is C (My favorite subjects in school are Spanish and mathematics).
4. The correct answer is H (book; I).
5. The correct answer is B (it's).

Practice FCAT Writing+ (Multiple-Choice)

1. The correct answer is A (Utensils). Details about a bowl, a mixer, and cookie sheets must be placed under the heading that groups them appropriately. Although a mixer could be listed under the subtopic "Mixing," cookie sheets would not fit. And only cookie sheets could possibly fit under the subtopic "Serving." Therefore, the only correct answer is Utensils.

2. The correct answer is H (a paper that describes the steps to baking good cookies). Elizabeth is planning to write a paper that describes because the subtopics listed are not persuasive, nor are they comparing anything. Her outline doesn't mention anything about being a good cook, either.

3. The correct answer is D (all of the above). Every detail listed, flour, eggs, and sugar, is included in an ingredient list for making cookies.

4. The correct answer is G (sentence 6). The word "appropreately" is spelled incorrectly. The correct spelling is "appropriately."

5. The correct answer C (the last one). The last sentence of the first paragraph loses focus. "I must have five posters of horses in my room" does not support the introduction of a topic about attending summer camp and learning how to care for horses.

6. The correct answer is I (sentence 12). This sentence presents an unrelated detail about having a horse in a two bedroom apartment, which does not support the main points of the essay about how much the student enjoyed learning how to take care of horses at summer camp.

7. The correct answer is C (to the end of paragraph 2). The sentence "I never could image that I would love an animal so much and so quickly" best concludes the paragraph in which Dawn is describing how much she loved the horse.

8. The correct answer is F (My experience at 4H camp has grown my love for horses). This sentence concludes the overall topic about how much Dawn loves horses because of her time at a 4H camp.

9. The correct answer is A (special: it's). The only choice that doesn't contain a sentence fragment is A.

10. The correct answer is F (their). Their is the possessive form of them, referring to the beaches that belong to the "groups and organizations."

11. The correct answer is A (beachgoers, residents and tourists alike), because the phrase between the commas describes the types of beachgoers but is not essential to the sentence. (If the information were essential, there would be no commas.)

12. The correct answer is H (Florida's beaches). The beaches "belong" to Florida, so an apostrophe + s is needed to show possession, and beaches is plural, meaning more than one beach.

13. The correct answer is B (She and I have the same algebra teacher). The only correct choice is the one that uses "She" because it is a pronoun that can be used as a subject of a sentence; "her" cannot.

14. The correct answer is F (The St. Johns River runs through the state of Florida) because it has correct capitalization. The "St. Johns River" and "Florida" are both proper nouns, but "state" is not a proper noun in this sentence.

15. The correct answer is A (She reads French and can speak it a little). This sentence has a compound predicate (two verbs joined by "and"), which does not require a comma.

16. The correct answer is G (The woman, who is a doctor, cares for her invalid father). The phrase "who is a doctor" is not essential to the meaning of the sentence and must be set apart from the sentence with commas.

17. The correct answer is C (Before everyone had a chance to study his notes, the teacher sprung a pop quiz on the class). "Everyone" is considered a singular (collective) noun and requires a singular pronoun, "his." ("His or her" would also be acceptable.)

18. The correct answer is F (The dog licked its wounds after fighting with the neighborhood cat). The correct spelling of "its" does not contain any apostrophes.

19. The correct answer is C (A bunch of grapes costs less than a bushel of apples). The singular subject "bunch" must have a singular verb "costs."

20. The correct answer is F (If the weather permits, then our playoff game will be held this afternoon). The only correct choice is F because it uses the "if . . . then" combination. "Than" is used in comparisons.

Chapter 5

Scoring

FCAT WRITING+ TEST (ESSAY) SCORES

Two evaluators will read your essay. They've been trained in how to score an essay, and they've been tested to see if they score according to the FCAT standards. Each evaluator scores your essay according to how well focused, organized, supported, and correct it is. Both of the evaluators' scores are then averaged. For example, if one evaluator scores your essay a 3 and the other gives you a 4, your official score will be 3.5. This is how it is possible to receive a score of 1.5, 2.5, 3.5, and so on.

In order to understand how essays are scored, you must look at examples of essays with different scores. After you finish learning the characteristics of each score, you will practice scoring three essays. By becoming aware of what a "6" looks like, you will be more likely to score well on the writing portion of the test.

Remember, even an essay given a score of a 6 is not a perfect essay. All responses are evaluated with the understanding that they are first drafts. This should take away some of the pressure during the testing.

Because four major components (as explained in Chapter 3) are considered when giving your essay a score, it is important to remember them when writing. Below you will find a brief list of the characteristics of each component you are expected to demonstrate in your essay, along with a sample persuasive essay given that score:

> **Tip:** Understand the scoring process so that you can give it your best try for a top score!

> **Tip:** Possible scores range from a "U" (unscorable) all the way to a "6."

A "6" Essay

An essay that earns 6 points may not be perfect, but it demonstrates all of the following:

FOCUS—has one thesis, and each paragraph has a clearly stated topic sentence

ORGANIZATION—has effective transitional devices between ideas

SUPPORT—is creative with detailed support that includes examples and statistics; precise wording and effective vocabulary are used

CONVENTIONS—has few (if any) mistakes in grammar or spelling; sentence structure is varied, may use creative writing strategies.

EXAMPLE OF A "6" ESSAY

In my opinion, I think that students should be allowed to take occasional field trips. They allow for students and teachers both to learn valuable lessons and enjoy themselves in the process. Most schools arrange trips that are intentionally educational. They make sure that there is a lesson learned while on the trip. If students and teachers combined, are trapped in the classroom all year long, it tends to get boring. They become uninteresting, and students set their attention on something else. If they allow for classes to take field trips, they are allowing us to learn from outside resources.

When schools arrange trips that are educational, they allow for a fun time while making sure that there is a lesson learned. For example, when classes go to different museums, they always learn something. Whether it be an art museum, a science museum, or a history museum, they will have a lesson learned while getting the adventure of a trip. I personally have been on many educational field trips that everyone enjoyed at the same time. When you go to a hands on museum, kids and teens have more fun.

To many students and teachers, being trapped in a classroom for a majority of the year makes them lose interest in learning. Students become bored with their work, and teachers get aggravated when the students begin to focus on other subjects. If they are allowed to travel and go on trips to learn it gains their attention back. They become more interested in the subject they are studying and may help them pay attention in the classroom again.

While some people may see field trips as people just being lazy and taking a free day, they need to see them as outside resources. We can use the trips as finding other ways to learn. If you go to places that are other than your school, you can look at things in different ways and get other opinions. It also offers a variety of point of views from a number of people and places.

As a conclusion, there are many ways that field trips are educational and not just a way to get out of doing work. Schools usually arrange trips that are already educational. Also students and teachers alike, can't stand being trapped in a classroom and school for a large portion of the year. Finally, when going on class trips, it offers for students to retrieve outside resources other than what their school may make available. These are reasons I believe many people will agree with me that field trips are used for educational reasons.

A "5" Essay

What separates an essay that earns 5 points from an essay that earns 6 points? The main difference is that it may have more errors than a "6" would and there is not as much variation and creativity as in a "6" essay. These are the major qualities of an essay that earns a score of 5:

FOCUS—has one thesis, and all paragraphs have a clear topic sentence

ORGANIZATION—is organized with appropriate transitions

SUPPORT—is supported with examples and statistics, as well as grade-level vocabulary

> CONVENTIONS—has some variation in sentence structure, and most conventions are followed; there may be a few minor spelling and/or grammar errors

EXAMPLE OF A "5" ESSAY

Field trips are valuable educational tools for students of all ages. During field trips, you can have a better hands-on learning experience than you could in the classroom. Field trips motivate students to become more interested in the topic that they are learning. Also, field trips provide a way for the students to get a break from the monotony of school.

Field trips are valuable educational tools because they give the students a better hands-on learning experience. When on field trips, students get to see what they are learning about up close and not through a textbook. Students have an opportunity to work with the subject matter without the teacher or instructor. Field trips can still be educational while allowing the student to have fun.

A good way to get a student interested in a topic is to go on a field trip. Becoming motivated about a subject plays a key role in how the student understands the material. Field trips might help some students to understand what they are learinig better. By giving the student an opportunity to see how the topic is used in real life, field trips enable him or her to relate to the subject in more depth than he or she would with a teacher.

School field trips are a way for students to take a break from school while still learning. Many field trips are educational and fun at the same time, allowing the student to learn without being in school. Also, the kids are more likely to grasp the material when they have fun memories of what their field trip was like.

In conclusion, field trips aren't always a waste of time. They give the students a much needed break from the classroom without them missing out on learning. Field trips give students a hands-on learning experience, motivate the students to do better in school, and give them a much needed break from the classroom.

A "4" Essay

An essay that earns a "4" is an above-average essay. These are the major qualities of an essay that earns a score of 4:

FOCUS—is focused with few (if any) unrelated ideas

ORGANIZATION—is organized, and basic transitions are used between ideas

SUPPORT—uses adequate choice of words, and some sentences are varied, but support is not detailed or specific

CONVENTIONS—generally follows most conventions but may have some spelling and/or grammar errors.

EXAMPLE OF A "4" ESSAY

Field trips are benefitial to schools. They give students a chance to have a break of school and have fun. A lot of field trips are educational. Field trips are chances for students and teachers to get to work together in a differnt sort of environment.

Field trips can be very educational. Last year I went on a field trip to a Civil War battlefield. At the battlefield we learned about differnt medicines that they used back then. There were people at differnt booths that taught you about differnt things that happened during the war. I learned things such as how they would sterilize wounds and what medical tools they would use.

After a while, students need a break of school and an opportunity to go somewhere differnt. We like having breaks from homework because it brings us back to school prepared and not overworked. Students like to go on field trips because it is a great experience. Field trips are fun.

Field trips are not only fun but educational. They aren't only fun to students, but teachers sometimes also enjoy them. Students like to have breaks every once in a while. A lot of field trips are not only fun, but are also educational. As you can see, field trips really are beneficial to schools.

A "3" Essay

An essay that earns a "3" is an average essay. Many students will earn this score on their essays. These are the major qualities of an essay that earns a score of 3:

FOCUS—is focused, but some ideas may stray from the main idea

ORGANIZATION—has some organization but may not be logical or have parts that are unorganized

SUPPORT—has support that is not developed, and word choice is adequate

CONVENTIONS—has some sentence structure variation and generally follows conventions but does have quite a few errors in spelling and grammar.

EXAMPLE OF A "3" ESSAY

Field trips are beneficial to a students, but in different ways, depending on the type of trip which is being taken. Some trips benefit students in that they can assist the student in their learning. Other trips do not benefit the student's education, but they may bring about other positive effects in the student, such as stress relief or social interaction. Also, weather it is beneficial or not depends on the student.

Some field trips benefit a student in the manner of enhancing their education. For example, some trips, such as one to Washington D.C. or to some natural or historical site may help them learn on certain topics with more ease as the learning experience would be more exciting and would grab a stronger hold on the student. Also, as these experiences can become fond memories, the knowledge aquired in that experience may be retained with the memory.

Other kinds of field trips benefit students in other ways. This kind of trip, a fun trip.

A "2" Essay

An essay that scores a "2" has the following major qualities:

FOCUS—does address topic but loses focus with extra information

ORGANIZATION—has some organization (like separate paragraphs or organization of ideas) but is brief

SUPPORT—support is not specific, with some ideas repeated, and word choice is limited or vague

CONVENTIONS—contains errors in conventions, with even some commonly used words spelled incorrectly.

EXAMPLE OF A "2" ESSAY

Field trips are valuable educational tools. They help students to learn things that would be impossible to learn inside the classroom, and they can also provide a hands on approach to learning.

First off field trips can help students to learn things that would be impossible to learn inside the classroom.

Next field trips can provide a hands on approach to learning. For instance, if a class was learning about marine life a class could go to the beach for a field trip to see actual examples.

Fild trips are valuable educational tools. They can help students to learn things that would be impossible to learn inside the classroom, and they can also provide a hands on approach to learning.

A "1" Essay

An essay rated "1" has the following major qualities:

FOCUS—addresses topic but loses focus with extra information included

ORGANIZATION—may have some organizational pattern but is not complete

SUPPORT—gives little if any support (or support is simply a list of generalizations) and has limited or inappropriate choice of words

CONVENTIONS—contains frequent errors in sentence structure and conventions, plus many commonly used words are spelled incorrectly.

EXAMPLE OF A "1" ESSAY

Some educators don't believe that field trip are educational and beneficial to the students that attend them. I believe that field trips are vital to the education process.

An Unscorable Essay

There are several reasons why a response is rated "unscorable":

The response is illegible, incorrect, and/or doesn't answer the prompt.

There is no response (writing folder is blank).

The response is simply the prompt rewritten or reworded with nothing else written about the topic.

SELF-SCORING RUBRIC

Included in this chapter is a self-scoring rubric. This is *not* the rubric that the evaluators will use for your FCAT essay. Because your essay is scored holistically, it is difficult to score your own writing without clear guidelines. Use the rubric below to learn the basic components of a good FCAT essay.

Directions: For each of the four scoring components, give yourself a score from 1 to 6. If the essay has demonstrated each trait listed below the component, write a 6; if half, a 3; if only one or two, a 1. Then take all four scores, add them together, and divide by 4. This is most likely the score the essay would receive if scored by an FCAT evaluator. Use this rubric to score the essays in this section or your own essays.

FOCUS _____

    one thesis statement giving one main idea or position
    introduction catches reader's attention
    each paragraph supports thesis
    conclusion restates main idea or position

CONVENTIONS _____

    correct spelling
    varied sentence structure
    complete sentences with no run-ons
    correct punctuation
    correct capitalization
    subject/verb agreement
    noun/pronoun agreement

SUPPORT _____

    at least two body paragraphs
    grade-level vocabulary
    avoids use of "things" and "stuff"
    vivid details (uses five senses)
    examples and statistics supporting main idea

ORGANIZATION _____

    topic sentence in each paragraph
    new paragraph for each topic sentence
    introduction
    conclusion

To determine the essay's overall score:

    _____ (Focus)
    + _____ (Organization)
    + _____ (Support)
    + _____ (Conventions)
    = _____ ÷ 4 = _____ (Overall Score)

PRACTICE

Now it's time to practice scoring three essays for the FCAT Writing+ Test (Essay). Read the essays below, decide what score each should receive, and briefly explain why. Use the previous rubric as your guide. Check your answers at the end of this chapter.

Essay 1: My Hero!

Everyone has a hero, whether it be a superhero, an actor or actress, anybody that they admire. In my case its my dad. he is the best man I know. He is always there, he is always helping and putting others before him, and he coaches for like everything.

One of the reasons my dad is my hero is because he is always there and just a good hearted person at soul. I play softball, volleyball, and flag football and when he can be he is always there cheering me on front row. He supports me in everything I do or want to do. If its the right thing of course. He taught me my right and wrongs and do's and don'ts. He always has good advice about anything you ask him. He also has a three hour story to go with it. Gotta love him.

Another reason my dad is my hero is because he is always helping and putting others before him. He'll do just about anything for anyone. I've learned alot watching him over the years. If it wasn't for the push my mom and dad give me to get good grades and put 110% in everything I do I wouldn't be who I am today.

The last reason my dad is my hero is he's so talented. He coach's girls fastpitch softball, flag football, and Pop Warner football. Last season my dad coached my brother, sisters and my flag football team. Talk about multi-tasking. He coached an undefeated girls softball team several times and football also. He's a great coach and I would reccomend him to anyone.

Those are some of the MANY reasons my dad is my hero. He is a great husband, father, and friend. After everything he does he still has time to keep a job and support his family. If we had more men like him America would be wonderful!

SCORE: _____

Reason for score:

Focus: _____

Organization: _____

Support: _____

Conventions: _____

Essay 2: The Effects of TV on Kids

When thinking of watching T.V. does the first thing that comes to your mind have anything to do with home work? Well proply not. Most kids spend hours watch T.V. But alot do homework and recieve good grades. But to much T.V. can be a problem to. I believe you should do your homework first, then watch  T.V. Priorites first, Right? Well its easy to say that now but when it comes time will you do it?

The effect T.V. has on kids these days ranges, there are many great shows that make kids happy and laugh, or teach you lessons or valueble information. But theres also alot of negative or bad shows that kids could really do without. When it comes to watching to much T.V. I think there should be a limit. kids should have to do homework first. Then watch T.V.

English, math, science, and hystory are the for main subjects in school. Not including all the electives and extra courses kids take. Even Elementry school does reading writing and science. So basicly every night kids get homework. But its hard because by the time kids get home from the 8 hour day all they wanna do is relax or they have to run off to sports or clubs.

SCORE: _____

Reason for score:

Focus: _____

Organization: _____

Support: _____

Conventions: _____

Essay 3

Volunteer work is one of the many things I believe students should have to do. I am in favor of it because it helps to make a better person out of the student and show their good side. I believe that only a certain number of hours should be needed because students do have alot to do. But they have 4 years to obtain the time to do it. It really shouldn't be that hard. It will also help show what students are slackers and which are not. Which students have more responsibilty then others, and it really helps out the community and society.

Students in highschool and even in middle school should all have to work doing community service. This will look very good on an application to collage, and will really help students see how important it is to help others. not only is it good for school but good for a person to. Most students only need 75 hours. That's really not much at all. I mean you go to high school for 4 years. What's 75 hours of your free time to help your community and yourself? You can get hours for doing practiclly anything: babysitting for free, helping the homeless, working at a shelter, teaching little kids, anything basiclly that you do for free to help others. It counts for school, and helps people in need. Thats why I think its imporatnt.

Another reason kids should have to do community service is to show responsibility. If a student cant obtain a small 75 hours of helping others out then how much time will they make to do other things in collage? Or help others in life? It also helps in teaching them not to be lazy and show some respect for others and there town. If students all get together they can really make a big difference. I believe that everyone should want to do community service, not have to do it. But it should be needed to graduate for students. I mean what can it hurt, yes they have alot of other things going on in there life but this is important for them as well.

Lastly, I believe that students should do it because its fun. They can really get together and work hard on building a playground or making dinner for someone, or reading to an elder, even having a car wash to raise money for something with all your friends! There is so much that can possibly be done that why not help? Students should earn credit for earning even more then the required amount of hours needed. Get a friend and do something good for you and your city or town. People will really appriecate it and it will show what a good responsible adult you will be.

In conclusion I believe that students should have at least 75 hours of community service. Without this students will not be as well informed with there community and people. It's a great thing to have for collage. Plus it will make them a more rounded and good person. Not only will they be helping themselves but also there community and fellow people. I think students should have to put a little time back into the town, and help all they can.

SCORE: _____

Reason for score:

Focus: _____

Organization: _____

Support: _____

Conventions: _____

FCAT READING TEST: SHORT-RESPONSE AND EXTENDED-RESPONSE ANSWERS

Tip: Partial credit will be given for any answer written in the space provided.

These answers will be not judged in the same manner as the essay. What is important is answering each question with as much support as you can. Imagine the reader of your responses is placing a checkmark over each detail you list that supports your answer. The more checkmarks, the better. Do not just write a bunch of words to fill up the space. And do not leave any of the answers blank.

Short-Response Rubric

2 points:

Student demonstrates complete understanding.

Support and/or examples are given.

Explanation is clear.

1 point:

Student demonstrates partial understanding.

General information is given simply.

0 points:

Response is illegible, incorrect, and/or doesn't answer the question/task.

EXAMPLE

From *The Tell-Tale Heart*
By Edgar Allen Poe

True! nervous, very, very dreadfully nervous I had been and am; but why will you say that I am mad? The disease had sharpened my senses, not destroyed, not dulled them. Above all was the sense of hearing acute. I heard all things in the heaven and in the earth. I heard many things in hell. How then am I mad?

Hearken! and observe how healthily, how calmly, I can tell you the whole story.

It is impossible to say how first the idea entered my brain, but, once conceived, it haunted me day and night. Object there was none. Passion there was none. I loved the old man. He had never wronged me. He had never given me insult. For his gold I had no desire. I think it was his eye! Yes, it was this! One of his eyes resembled that of a vulture—a pale blue eye with a film over it. Whenever it fell upon me my blood ran cold, and so by degrees, very gradually, I made up my mind to take the life of the old man, and thus rid myself of the eye for ever.

READ/THINK/EXPLAIN: What justification does the narrator give for wanting to murder the old man?

Response: *The narrator has decided to murder the old man simply because of the old man's evil eye. The narrator believes the eye resembles a vulture. Also, the narrator says that the eye causes his "blood to run cold." This probably means he gets a chill from seeing the eye. Also, the narrator simply wants to be rid of the evil eye forever and believes the only way to get rid of it is to kill the old man.*

SCORE: 2. This response deserves full credit because it answers the question completely and correctly; also, it gives details to support the position.

Extended-Response Rubric

4 points:

  Student demonstrates complete understanding.

  Support and/or examples are given.

  Explanation is clear.

  Text-based answer is given.

3 points:

Student demonstrates understanding with an accurate response.

Answer is not detailed or supported fully with examples from the reading passage.

2 points:

Student demonstrates partial understanding.

Response is correct, but too general.

Support and/or examples are omitted.

1 point:

Answer is incomplete

0 points:

Response is illegible, incorrect, and/or doesn't answer the question/task.

EXAMPLE

The Declaration of Independence

We hold these Truths to be self-evident, that all Men are created equal, that they are endowed, by their creator, with certain unalienable Rights, that among these are Life, Liberty, and the Pursuit of Happiness. That to secure these Rights, Governments are instituted among Men, deriving their just Powers from the Consent of the Governed, that whenever any Form of Government becomes destructive of these Ends, it is the Right of the People to alter or to abolish it, and to institute new Government, laying its Foundation on such Principles, and organizing its Powers in such Form, as to them shall seem most likely to effect their Safety and Happiness. Prudence, indeed, will dictate, that Governments long established,

IN CONGRESS. July 4, 1776.

The unanimous Declaration ... States of America,

should not be changed for light and transient Causes; and accordingly all Experience hath shewn, that Mankind are more disposed to suffer, while Evils are sufferable, than to right themselves by abolishing the Forms to which they are accustomed. But when a long Train of Abuses and Usurpations, pursuing invariably the same Object, evinces a Design to reduce them under absolute Despotism, it is their Right, it is their Duty, to throw off such Government, and to provide new Guards for their future Security. Such has been the patient Sufferance of these Colonies; and such is now the Necessity which constrains them to alter their former Systems of Government. The History of the present King of Great-Britain is a History of repeated Injuries and Usurpations, all having in direct Object the Establishment of an absolute Tyranny over these States. To prove this, let Facts be submitted to a candid World.

READ/THINK/EXPLAIN: Explain the three unalienable rights that all men have under the Declaration of Independence.

Response: *The three unalienable rights that all men have according to the Declaration of Independence are "life, liberty, and the pursuit of happiness." These rights are protected because the writers believed that these rights should not be taken away. Basically, everyone has the right to live. Therefore, it is against the law commit murder, which would be taking away someone's life. The other right we have is the right to liberty. This means we are provided many freedoms like the freedom to practice any religion and the freedom to speak. The final right we have is the right to "pursue happiness." This covers such tasks as being able to start a business.*

SCORE: 4
This essay correctly identifies the three rights outlined in the Declaration of Independence. Then it goes on to explain them in more detail with support from the text. The answer does not stray from the topic or the text, either.

PRACTICE

Now it's time to practice scoring several FCAT Reading Test responses, short and extended. Read the reading passages (or excerpts) and sample answers below. Then decide what score each should receive and briefly explain why. Use the previous rubrics as your guide. Check your answers at the end of this chapter.

The Inventions of Thomas A. Edison

Thomas A. Edison was a great inventor. Because he has changed the way most American's live their daily lives, he has made a great contribution to our country, especially with three of his most famous inventions.

Making him instantly famous, Edison's invention of the phonograph changed the lives of Americans and others around the world. While trying to improve the telegraph, he actually ended up creating a device that recorded sound onto a tinfoil cylinder with needles. Transitioning onto flat disks from Edison's cylinders has proven to be very compact and efficient. Today, we can thank Edison for all of the gadgets we use today that stem from his invention like compact discs.

Another invention that changed the lives of Americans is the lightbulb. Looking for a practical, safe, and affordable light, Edison improved an existing idea for light and the result was the lightbulb as we know it. This is an invention that we take for granted every day. By producing a reliable light source that lasted a long time, Edison earned new fame.

Most people don't know, but we can credit Edison with his contribution to the movies. Also in the late 1800s, he invented a camera (also known as the kinetoscope) for motion pictures. Not soon after he invented this camera, he developed a device named the projectoscope. This invention was used in the first movie theater in New York.

Edison was truly a genius. His inventions have evolved over time. It's probably safe to say that every American has been affected by Edison's inventions.

READ/THINK/EXPLAIN: What devices today probably are modern versions of Edison's earlier inventions?

Short Response 1

Today, we have CD/DVD burners which are probably the modern equivalent to the phonograph. You can copy and record to the CD just like you could using the phonograph. Although the light bulb has not changed that much from the late 1800s, there are different types of bulbs now that are even more efficient in burning electricity: incandescent lights. The final modern-day equivalent to one of Edison's invention of the projectoscope would be any equipment that large movie directors and theaters use.

SCORE: _____

Reason for score:

Focus: _____

Organization: _____

Support: _____

Conventions: _____

READ/THINK/EXPLAIN: In what ways have Edison's inventions changed our lives today?

Extended Response 2

Without Edison's inventions, life as we know it would be very different. We wouldn't be able to record and play back our favorite songs. Instead we would only be able to hear music live. Another consequence of not being able to record would be that we probably wouldn't even have the computer! Edison's technology for recording truly paved the way for all forms of recording. A musician probably owes a lot to Edison because they are able to record their music and sell it to everyone in the world. In addition to music recordings, another invention, the electric light bulb has also changed the way we live. Being able to read or do activities in our homes after the sun has gone down is very much safer today—no more candles and accidental fires. The final improvement in our lives today thanks to Edison is movies! We are able to watch movies even at home, just as well as we can see them on the front lines. Overall, without Edison, we would be without so many of the enjoyments of life.

SCORE: _____

Reason for score:

Focus: _____

Organization: _____

Support: _____

Conventions: _____

The Runaway
By Robert Frost

Once when the snow of the year was beginning to fall,
We stopped by a mountain pasture to say "Whose colt?"
A little Morgan had one forefoot on the wall,
The other curled at his breast. He dipped his head
And snorted at us. And then he had to bolt.
We heard the miniature thunder where he fled,
And we saw him, or thought we saw him, dim and grey,
Like a shadow against the curtain of falling flakes.
"I think the little fellow's afraid of the snow.
He isn't winter-broken. It isn't play
With the little fellow at all. He's running away.
I doubt if even his mother could tell him, 'Sakes,
It's only weather.' He'd think she didn't know!
Where is his mother? He can't be out alone."
And now he comes again with a clatter of stone
And mounts the wall again with whited eyes
And all his tail that isn't hair up straight.
He shudders his coat as if to throw off flies.
"Whoever it is that leaves him out so late,
When other creatures have gone to stall and bin,
Ought to be told to come and take him in."

READ/THINK/EXPLAIN:
Give examples of imagery from this poem, and explain how they help the reader to experience the poem. Use details and information from the poem to explain your answer.

Short Response 3

Frost uses many different examples of imagery in this poem. One example is the description of "the miniature thunder where he fled" helps the reader to better experience the poem by "hearing" the colt. Using imagery definitely helps the reader experience the poem through his senses.

SCORE: _____

Reason for score:

Focus: _____

Organization: _____

Support: _____

Conventions: _____

READ/THINK/EXPLAIN: What is the theme or central message of this poem? Use details and information from the story to explain your answer.

Extended Response 4

I believe the theme of this poem is do not run away from your problems. Frost uses personification to make the horse seem like a human running away from his problems. The horse could be compared to a young child running away who ends up facing even greater fears.

SCORE: _____

Reason for score:

Focus: _____

Organization: _____

Support: _____

Conventions: _____

TIPS FOR TEACHERS

■ Use classroom time for peer editing and scoring practice. Students will most likely score higher when they truly understand how to score an essay properly. If they know how to spot a "6" essay, they are more likely to be able to write one!

■ Use student samples (without names) as examples on the overhead. Let students try to guess what score that essay would receive. You don't have to use that class's work; you could use the previous year's work or another class period's work to avoid any embarrassment.

■ Spend time talking about how to improve an essay. Show students an essay that received a 3 or below, then ask them to rewrite the same essay improving it by at least one point.

■ Before students turn in an essay, have them write what score they think their essay should receive and why.

■ Make copies of the "self-scoring" rubric. Use them to grade your students' essays throughout the year. This way they will be familiar with the basic elements they must include in their essays. It will also give them a general indication of how they will score on actual test day.

TIPS FOR PARENTS

■ Familiarize yourself with the different processes for scoring the writing and reading tests. Become proficient in recognizing an essay of 3 or above. Look through your child's papers and find essays you believe he or she could improve to the next level.

■ Encourage your child to read at home. Reading good literature will aid your child in understanding how to vary sentence structure and will improve your child's vocabulary.

■ Because reading many different types of writing will also help your child's reading comprehension, read the newspaper together! Enjoy discussing the editorials, or even the music page. Sometimes a local story may catch your child's interest and provide a great time of discussion and higher level thinking.

■ Practice scoring your child's essays that he or she writes in response to the practice in this book. You will learn how to better encourage and instruct your child in scoring well on the final test.

ANSWERS

FCAT Writing+ Test (Essay) Practice

Essay 1

Score: 4

This essay received a score of 4 because it is organized logically. Also, it is focused and stays on the topic throughout. There are many details listed about what exactly the student's dad does, but the details do not have much depth. There are approximately 7 spelling errors and 12 grammar errors.

Essay 2

Score: 2

This essay received a score of 2 because it has no clear thesis statement. In fact, it states two different opinions about the effects of TV in the first paragraph. There is little to no organization. Besides having few or no transitions between ideas, the conclusion is missing. Another supporting paragraph is necessary, too. There are no examples of what lessons are taught or what valuable information is given on TV. Although the last paragraph gives many details, these details do not support the thesis well. There are also many problems with the conventions in this essay because not one sentence is free of errors.

Essay 3
Score: 5

This essay received a score of a 5 because it has specific, relevant details and has organized details, but it lacks some transitions. The essay does have variety in its sentence structure and uses some specific word choices. It does, however, contain some errors in grammar and conventions, but the errors do not interfere with understanding. Overall, the essay clearly states a position and persuades the reader to that point of view.

FCAT Reading Test Practice
Response 1
Score: 2

This short response received a score of 2 out of 2 possible points because the student demonstrated complete understanding of the topic. The student gave specific examples of modern day devices that have come from Edison's inventions, being careful to cover all three main types. The information is clear and easy to understand and is based on the text.

Response 2
Score: 4

This extended response received a score of 4 out of 4 possible points because the student demonstrated complete understanding of the topic. The student explained how Edison's inventions have specifically changed our lives today. The student also referred in the article to the three main inventions of Edison throughout the response. The explanation is clear and logical, based on the text.

Response 3

Score: 1

This short response received a score of 1 out of 2 possible points because it demonstrates only a partial understanding of the question. The information and examples are too general to earn a higher score. The student should have given several more examples of imagery in the answer, like the following sentence: When Frost writes, "like a shadow against the curtain of falling flakes," the reader can better picture what the colt must have looked like against the falling snow.

Response 4

Score: 1

This extended response received a score of 1 out of 4 possible points because it does not elaborate and give examples from the text. The student should have included more information about the theme supported by details from the text.

Appendix

OVERVIEW OF FLORIDA SUNSHINE STATE BENCHMARKS

The current Sunshine State Standards are currently under review and will be revised by 2007.

Reading Benchmarks

LA.A.1.3.1. The student uses background knowledge of the subject and text structure knowledge to make complex predictions of content, purpose, and organization.

LA.A.1.3.2. The student uses a variety of strategies to analyze words and text, draw conclusions, use context and word structure clues, and recognize organizational patterns.

LA.A.1.3.3. The student demonstrates consistent and effective use of interpersonal and academic vocabularies in reading, writing, listening, and speaking.

LA.A.1.3.4. The student uses strategies to clarify meaning, such as rereading, note taking, summarizing, outlining, and writing a grade level–appropriate report.

LA.A.2.2.2. The student identifies the author's purpose in a simple text.

LA.A.2.2.3. The student recognizes when a text is primarily intended to persuade.

LA.A.2.2.7. The student recognizes the use of comparison and contrast in a text.

LA.A.2.3.1. The student determines the main idea or essential message in a text and identifies relevant details and facts and patterns of organization.

LA.A.2.3.2. The student identifies the author's purpose and/or point of view in a variety of texts and uses the information to construct meaning.

LA.A.2.3.3. The student recognizes logical, ethical, and emotional appeals in texts.

LA.A.2.3.4. The student uses a variety of reading materials to develop personal preferences in reading.

LA.A.2.3.5. The student locates, organizes, and interprets written information for a variety of purposes, including classroom research, collaborative decision making, and performing a school or real-world task.

LA.A.2.3.6 The student uses a variety of reference materials, including indexes, magazines, newspapers, and journals, and tools, including card catalogs and computer catalogs, to gather information for research projects.

LA.A.2.3.7. The student synthesizes and separates collected information into useful components using a variety of techniques, such as source cards, note cards, spreadsheets, and outlines.

Literature Benchmarks

LA.E.1.3.1. The student identifies the defining characteristics of classic literature, such as timelessness, dealing with universal themes and experiences, and communicating across cultures.

LA.E.1.3.2. The student recognizes complex elements of plot, including setting, character development, conflicts, and resolutions.

LA.E.1.3.3. The student understands various elements of authors' craft appropriate at this grade level, including word choice, symbolism, figurative language, mood, irony, foreshadowing, flashback, persuasion techniques, and point of view in both fiction and non-fiction.

LA.E.1.3.4. The student knows how mood or meaning is conveyed in poetry, such as word choice, dialect, invented words, concrete or abstract terms, sensory or figurative language, use of sentence structure, line length, punctuation, and rhythm.

LA.E.1.3.5. The student identifies common themes in literature.

LA.E.2.2.1. The student recognizes cause-and-effect relationships in literary texts. [Applies to fiction, non-fiction, poetry, and drama.]

LA.E.2.3.1. The student understands how character and plot development, point of view, and tone are used in various selections to support a central conflict or story line.

LA.E.2.3.2. The student responds to a work of literature by interpreting selected phrases, sentences, or passages and applying the information to personal life.

LA.E.2.3.3. The student knows that a literary text may elicit a wide variety of valid responses.

LA.E.2.3.4. The student knows ways in which literature reflects the diverse voices of people from various backgrounds.

LA.E.2.3.5. The student recognizes different approaches that can be applied to the study of literature, including thematic approaches change, personal approaches such as what an individual brings to his or her study of literature, historical approaches such as how a piece of literature reflects the time period in which it was written.

LA.E.2.3.6. The student identifies specific questions of personal importance and seeks to answer them through literature.

LA.E.2.3.7. The student identifies specific interests and the literature that will satisfy those interests.

LA.E.2.3.8. The student knows how a literary selection can expand or enrich personal viewpoints or experiences.

GRAPHIC ORGANIZERS FOR WRITING THE ESSAY

Use the following pages to practice different types of organizers for your FCAT Writing+ (Essay) Test. Remember, when you plan your writing, it will be more focused and organized, bringing up your score on the FCAT.

Cause/Effect

This type of graphic organizer is mainly used to organize thoughts for an essay that will explain the causes or effects of a certain action.

Start with your topic at the top of the chart—this is either the cause following which you will describe the effects OR an effect with possible causes. If you list the cause at the top first (more common), then list the effects in the next few boxes in the chart. If you list an effect first, then list the possible causes.

Inside the boxes make sure you have at least two or three examples or subtopics for your topic. More might make your topic lose focus, and fewer will not support your main idea enough. Each box represents a paragraph but don't forget to write a concluding paragraph summarizing your main points.

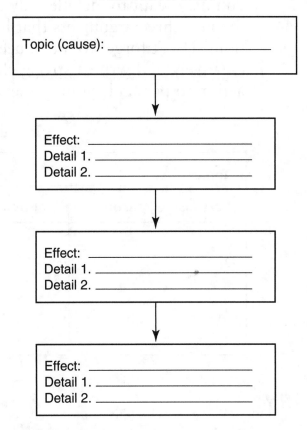

Cause/Effect Chart

Topic (cause): _____

Effect: _____
Detail 1. _____
Detail 2. _____

Effect: _____
Detail 1. _____
Detail 2. _____

Effect: _____
Detail 1. _____
Detail 2. _____

T-chart

This type of graphic organizer is mainly used to organize thoughts for a persuasive topic.

Start by writing your topic (or more specifically, which side of the topic you will argue persuasively in your essay) at the top of the chart on the line provided.

On the left-hand side, list reasons to support the point of view you've chosen for your topic. On the right-hand side, anticipate the arguments people could make against your reasons. By preparing in advance for possible arguments, you will be more persuasive in your argument.

This organizer shows a place for five reasons; however, you may want to include only three. Or, you may choose the best three arguments that have weak potential objections. Don't forget to introduce your topic to the reader creatively and write a strong closing argument or call to action to persuade your audience.

T-chart

Topic: _____	
Persuasive Reason	**Possible Arguments Against**
1.	
2.	
3.	
4.	
5.	

GLOSSARY

Audience: the intended reader(s) of your essay.

Body: support for your main idea with reasons and examples.

Brainstorm: to list anything that comes to mind about your topic.

Call to action: in a persuasive essay, the concluding sentence that urges the reader to take action.

Clincher: in an expository essay, the concluding sentence that leaves a lasting impression on the reader.

Conclusion: the last paragraph in your essay that summarizes the main points and restates your thesis.

Conventions: basic writing skills, like spelling, punctuation, and grammar.

Directions for writing: how to focus your topic so that you do not write about more than one subject.

Editing: correcting and revising your essay.

Expository: explaining why or how with support and details.

Focus: one main idea; everything in the essay relates to this one idea in some way.

Holistic: looking at the entire essay, not just individual parts. (This is the way your Writing+ Test (Essay) will be scored.)

Hook: an opening sentence that captures the reader's attention and makes him or her want to read more.

Imagery: vivid descriptions based on the five senses (sight, smell, touch, sound, taste).

Introduction: the first paragraph in your essay that presents the main idea to the reader.

Main idea: an idea that supports the thesis of a paper; each paragraph of an essay should have only one main idea.

Map: a visual grouping of main ideas centered around one thesis, with supporting details connected to the main ideas.

Metaphor: a comparison without the use of "like" or "as."

Organization: arrangement of details in a logical order; grouping similar topics together.

Outline: to organize your thoughts and ideas into a list with topics and subtopics.

Personification: giving human qualities to animals or objects.

Persuasive: intending to convince someone to believe a certain point of view.

Prompt: a general topic assigned for you to write about in your essay.

Proofread: rereading your work and checking it for errors in spelling, capitalization, punctuation, and so on.

Roman numeral: a capital letter used to represent a number. (For example, "I" represents 1; and "II" represents 2.)

Score: the grade you earn, between 1 and 6, on the essay, with 6 being the highest score possible.

Simile: a comparison using the word "like" or "as."

Support: examples or details that strengthen your point of view or your main point.

Thesis statement: a statement that summarizes what the entire essay is about by stating your point of view and how you will support that view.

Tone: the author's attitude revealed in setting or characterization (also known as the mood).

Topic: the subject of a paper.

Topic sentence: a sentence that makes the main point of a paragraph in one statement.

Transition: a word or phrase that moves a topic from one idea to the next in a smooth manner.

Web: a visual grouping of main ideas centered around one thesis, with supporting details connected to the main ideas.

Writing situation: the specific topic assigned to you for your essay.

SELF-REFLECTION

After you have completed the Practice FCAT Tests, look over your results and answer the following questions.

1. In what areas are you strong? _____

_____

_____

_____

_____

2. Besides completing the practice exams in this book, what will you do to continue to strengthen yourself in these areas? _____

_____

_____

_____

3. In what areas are you weak? _____

_____

_____

_____

4. Besides completing the practice exams in this book, what will you do to work in these areas? _____

_____

_____

_____

5. What scores did you give yourself on the short-response and extended-response questions? Why?

_____

_____

_____

6. What score did you give yourself on the FCAT Writing+ Test (Essay)? Why? _____

_____

_____

_____

7. Give your written responses (short response, extended response, and essay) to at least two people to read and score (according to the given rubrics). What scores did they give you? Were they the same scores you gave yourself? Why or why not? _____

_____

_____

_____

_____

8. Write your specific plan to prepare for the FCAT here:

_____

_____

_____

_____

WEB SITES

For Students

http://www.fcatexplorer.com/
FCAT Explorer provides practice with the Sunshine State Standards. A sign-in name and password are required (ask your school for this information).

http://www.firn.edu/doe/sas/fcat.htm
This is the FCAT home page sponsored by the Florida Department of Education. Here you can find links to all state-sponsored FCAT information.

http://www.nova.edu/~bsonja/
This web site includes a guide to the FCAT, a simulation for testing, preparation activities, and more.

http://www.brainchild.com/gen/usmap.asp
This web site includes an online assessment that you can take for practice. Click on Florida and follow the links to FCAT Reading Test practice.

For Parents*

http://www.fcatexplorer.com/
FCAT Explorer helps students practice with the Sunshine State Standards. There is a management system for teachers or parents that tracks a student's performance. A sign-in name and password are required (ask your child's school for this information).

http://www.firn.edu/doe/sas/fcat.htm
This is the FCAT home page sponsored by the Florida Department of Education. Here you can find links to all state-sponsored FCAT information.

http://www.nova.edu/~bsonja/
This web site includes a guide to the FCAT, a simulation for testing, preparation activities, and more.

http://florida-family.net/SAC/fcat-testing.htm
This web site gives information on the basics of the FCAT.

For Teachers

http://www.fcatexplorer.com/
FCAT Explorer helps students practice with the Sunshine State Standards. There is a management system for teachers or parents that tracks a student's performance. A sign-in name and password are required (your administration should be able to provide this information).

http://www.firn.edu/doe/sas/fcat.htm
This is the FCAT home page sponsored by the Florida Department of Education. Here you can find links to all state-sponsored FCAT information.

*Many school districts have FCAT information available. Ask your child's teacher what other help and information are available to you.

http://www.nova.edu/~bsonja/
This web site includes a guide to the FCAT, a simulation for testing, preparation activities, and more.

http://osi.fsu.edu/
This is the site for the Office of School Improvement (OSI) at the Florida Department of Education (DOE). Use the searchable database of FCAT sites to find more information.

http://www.ibinder.uwf.edu/steps/welcome.cfm
This site created by the University of West Florida College of Professional Studies and the Panhandle Area Center for Educational Enhancement provides professional development resources including activities based on the Sunshine State Standards.

http://www.readnwritenaturally.org/
Reading and Writing Naturally is a searchable database of children's literature. The literature included is related to the environment and linked to Florida Sunshine State Standards.

http://www.fsdb.kl2.fl.us/curric/sss.html
This site contains an Electronic Curriculum Planning Tool related to the Sunshine State Standards.

http://www.firn.edu/doe/sas/fcat/pdf/fcatguid.pdf
This Florida DOE FCAT site specifically explains what every teacher should know about the FCAT.

http://www.sbac.edu/~lms/FCAT.htm
This web site guides educators in how to understand the FCAT, with suggestions for test preparation.

http://www.sarasota.k12.fl.us/MRC/tchngreadngmain.htm
This web site covers the challenges of teaching students to read, as well as how to score well on the FCAT. You will find information on assessment and evaluation, the reading process, choosing appropriate texts, and more.

READING STRATEGIES BOOKMARK

Directions: Cut the bookmark on this page and use it as a reminder for the reading strategies you learned in Chapter 2.

Reading Strategies

- Underline main ideas once.

- Underline supporting details and examples two times.

- Circle unfamiliar words.

- Box dates and numbers.

- Write a brief summary.

BARRON'S
GRADE 8
FCAT
IN READING AND WRITING PLUS

PRACTICE AND REVIEW IN—
All test areas, supplemented with additional
practice questions and answers

TEST-TAKING ADVICE
How to read and understand test questions
plus two full-length practice exams with
thorough answers and explanations

KELLEY BATTLES

Index

FCAT Practice Test One

FCAT READING TEST

Read the article "The History of Hurricanes" before answering questions 1 through 7 in the P1: FCAT Reading Test answer book.

The History of Hurricanes

Scientists have only been studying hurricanes for about 100 years. But there is evidence of hurricanes occurring long in the past. For example, geologists (scientists who study the earth) believe that layers of sediment in a lake in Alabama [were] brought there by a hurricane in the Gulf of Mexico as long as 3,000 years ago! There is also evidence in Florida of hurricanes more than 1,000 years ago.

One of the first human records of hurricanes appears in Mayan hieroglyphics. The Mayans also practiced a kind of mitigation and risk reduction* by building their major settlements away from the hurricane-prone coastline. In fact, it is the

---

* To practice "mitigation and risk reduction" means to act in such a way that would have fewer consequences (for example, to build homes that can withstand hurricanes).

GO ON →

©Copyright 2006 by Barron's Educational Series, Inc.

Mayan word *Hurakan* that became our word "hurricane." Hurakan was the name of one of their gods, who, they believed, blew his breath across the water and brought forth dry land. Later, Carib Indians gave the name "Hurican" to one of their gods of evil.

Many storms left important marks on history. In 1565, a hurricane scattered a French fleet of war ships and allowed the Spanish to capture a French fort in what is now Florida. In 1609, a fleet of ships carrying settlers from England to Virginia was struck by a hurricane. Some of the ships were damaged and part of the fleet grounded on Bermuda, an island nation in the Atlantic. These passengers became the first people to live on Bermuda. In 1640, a hurricane partially destroyed a large Dutch fleet that was poised to attack Cuba.

There were a number of particularly severe hurricanes as the U.S. went from the 1800s to the 1900s. Hurricanes hit Louisiana, South Carolina and Georgia in 1893 and killed as many as 4,000 people. In 1900, a famous Texas hurricane killed more than 8,000 people and was a Category 4 storm.

As forecasting improved communities were no longer surprised by hurricanes and could take measures to evacuate ahead of the storm. While destruction continued, the number of deaths in hurricanes dropped significantly.

—*Hurricane Research Division of the Atlantic Oceanographic and Meteorological Laboratory/NOAA*

Base your answers to questions 1 through 7 on the article "The History of Hurricanes."

1. From the article about hurricanes, the reader can conclude that scientists have been researching hurricanes
   A. since Mayan times.
   B. only for the past 100 years.
   C. only for the past 1,000 years.
   D. for the past 3,000 years.

GO ON →

2. The article implies that hurricanes have been
   F. known to be discovered by the Mayans.
   G. increasing in strength over the last 100 years.
   H. decreasing in strength over the last 100 years.
   I. a destructive force over the history of humanity.

3. Read the following sentence from the article:

   Some of the ships were damaged and part of the fleet grounded on Bermuda, an island nation in the Atlantic.

   The word "fleet" means
   A. a military organization.
   B. a warship.
   C. many ships.
   D. the bottom section of a ship.

4. What is the author's purpose in writing this article about hurricanes?
   F. to give a brief history of hurricanes
   G. to explain the different types of hurricanes
   H. to illustrate the destruction of hurricanes
   I. to define hurricanes according to the Mayans

5. Look at the chart below.

Saffir–Simpson Hurricane Scale

- **Tropical Storm**—winds 39–73 mph

- **Category 1 Hurricane**—winds 74–95 mph
  No real damage to buildings. Damage to unanchored mobile homes. Some damage to poorly constructed signs. Also, some coastal flooding and minor pier damage.

- **Category 2 Hurricane**—winds 96–110 mph
  Some damage to building roofs, doors, and windows. Considerable damage to mobile homes. Flooding damages piers, and small craft in unprotected moorings may break their moorings. Some trees blown down.

©Copyright 2006 by Barron's Educational Series, Inc.

GO ON →

- **Category 3 Hurricane**—winds 111–130 mph
  Some structural damage to small residences and utility buildings. Large trees blown down. Mobile homes and poorly built signs destroyed. Flooding near the coast destroys smaller structures, with larger structures damaged by floating debris. Terrain may be flooded well inland.

- **Category 4 Hurricane**—winds 131–155 mph
  More extensive curtainwall failures with some complete roof structure failure on small residences. Major erosion of beach areas. Terrain may be flooded well inland.

- **Category 5 Hurricane**—winds 156 mph and up
  Complete roof failure on many residences and industrial buildings. Some complete building failures with small utility buildings blown over or away. Flooding causes major damage to lower floors of all structures near the shoreline. Massive evacuation of residential areas may be required.

According to the article and the Saffir–Simpson Scale, the famous Texas hurricane that killed more than 8,000 people had sustained winds of
A. 96 to 110 mph.
B. 111 to 130 mph.
C. 131 to 155 mph.
D. 156 mph and up.

6. According to the Saffir-Simpson Scale, how are Category 1 and Category 5 hurricanes different?
F. Category 1 hurricanes do less damage than Category 5 hurricanes.
G. The only difference is in the wind speed.
H. Only Category 1 hurricanes produce major flooding.
I. Category 5 hurricanes do not require massive evacuation of coastal areas.

7. READ/THINK/ EXPLAIN: How have hurricanes affected civilization over time? Use details and information from the article to support your answer.

Read the poem "Paul Revere's Ride" before answering questions 8 through 16.

Paul Revere's Ride

By Henry Wadsworth Longfellow

1 Listen my children and you shall
hear
Of the midnight ride of Paul
Revere,
On the eighteenth of April, in
Seventy-five;
Hardly a man is now alive
Who remembers that famous day
and year.

2   He said to his friend, "If the
British march
By land or sea from the town to-
night,
Hang a lantern aloft in the belfry
arch
Of the North Church tower as a
signal light,—
One if by land, and two if by sea;
And I on the opposite shore will
be,
Ready to ride and spread the
alarm
Through every Middlesex village
and farm,
For the country folk to be up and
to arm."

3 Then he said "Good-night!" and
with muffled oar
Silently rowed to the Charlestown
shore,
Just as the moon rose over the
bay,
Where swinging wide at her
moorings lay

4 The Somerset, British man-of-war;
A phantom ship, with each mast
and spar
Across the moon like a prison bar,
And a huge black hulk, that was
magnified
By its own reflection in the tide.
Meanwhile, his friend through
alley and street

©Copyright 2006 by Barron's Educational Series, Inc.

GO ON →

Wanders and watches, with eager ears,
Till in the silence around him he hears
The muster of men at the barrack door,
The sound of arms, and the tramp of feet,
And the measured tread of the grenadiers,
Marching down to their boats on the shore.

5 Then he climbed the tower of the Old North Church,
By the wooden stairs, with stealthy tread,
To the belfry chamber overhead,
And startled the pigeons from their perch
On the sombre rafters, that round him made
Masses and moving shapes of shade,—
By the trembling ladder, steep and tall,
To the highest window in the wall,
Where he paused to listen and look down
A moment on the roofs of the town

And the moonlight flowing over all.

6 Beneath, in the churchyard, lay the dead,
In their night encampment on the hill,
Wrapped in silence so deep and still
That he could hear, like a sentinel's tread,
The watchful night-wind, as it went
Creeping along from tent to tent,
And seeming to whisper, "All is well!"
A moment only he feels the spell
Of the place and the hour, and the secret dread
Of the lonely belfry and the dead;
For suddenly all his thoughts are bent
On a shadowy something far away,
Where the river widens to meet the bay,—
A line of black that bends and floats
On the rising tide like a bridge of boats.

GO ON →

Base your answers to questions 8 through 16 on the poem "Paul Revere's Ride."

8. Read the first few lines from the second stanza:

> He said to his friend, "If the British march
> By land or sea from the town to-night,
> Hang a lantern aloft in the belfry arch
> Of the North Church tower as a signal light,—

The word *"aloft"* means
A. inside.
B. above.
C. beside.
D. under.

9. Read these lines from stanza 6:

> Beneath, in the churchyard, lay the dead,
> In their night encampment on the hill,
> Wrapped in silence so deep and still

Who lies dead in the churchyard?
F. the men who were killed by the Americans from a previous war
G. the men and women who were killed by the British during the night
H. the men and women buried in the cemetery
I. the ancestors of the British who were buried there many years ago

10. What is the author's purpose in writing this poem?
A. to encourage the reader to look up more information on Paul Revere
B. to demonstrate to the reader the effects of war on a small town
C. to inform the reader of the famous midnight ride of Paul Revere by entertaining
D. to prove to the reader that Paul Revere is the most famous of all soldiers in American history

11. What is Paul Revere's main goal in the poem?
F. to tell his friend how many lanterns to hang in the belfry arch
G. to ride his horse to the shore to see if the British are coming
H. to inform the British that the Americans are coming
I. to alarm the people that the British are coming

©Copyright 2006 by Barron's Educational Series, Inc.

GO ON →

12. Why is Paul Revere in such a hurry?

   A. He is worried that someone else will take his fame from him

   B. He must warn his countrymen that the enemy has arrived during the night so that they are not killed in their sleep and lose the war

   C. He must finish his ride before midnight or his friend won't be there to see the signal

   D. He must warn the British that the Americans are ready for them to attack

13. Which statement best characterizes Paul Revere's attitude toward the British?

   F. The British are Revere's enemy.

   G. Revere is anxiously waiting the arrival of the British.

   H. Revere doesn't want his friend to know that he is meeting the British.

   I. Revere is ready to fight the British as soon as they come ashore.

14. READ/THINK/ EXPLAIN: Read these few lines from stanza 5:

By the trembling ladder, steep and tall,
To the highest window in the wall,
Where he paused to listen and look down
A moment on the roofs of the town
And the moonlight flowing over all.

How does this quotation reveal the mood of Paul Revere's friend? Use details and examples from the poem to support your answer.

15. This poem can best be described as

   A. informative.

   B. persuasive.

   C. expository.

   D. narrative.

16. READ/THINK/ EXPLAIN: How do rhyme and rhythm contribute to the development of the poem? Use details and examples from the poem to support your answer.

GO ON →

Read the excerpt from "The Gift of the Magi" before answering questions 17 through 27.

The Gift of the Magi

By O. Henry

At 7 o'clock the coffee was made and the frying pan was on the back of the stove hot and ready to cook the chops.

Jim was never late. Della doubled the fob chain in her hand and sat on the corner of the table near the door that he always entered. Then she heard his step on the stair away down on the first flight, and she turned white for just a moment. She had a habit for saying little silent prayer about the simplest every-day things, and now she whispered:

"Please God, make him think I am still pretty."

The door opened and Jim stepped in and closed it. He looked thin and very serious. Poor fellow, he was only twenty-two—and to be burdened with a family! He needed a new overcoat and he was without gloves.

Jim stopped inside the door, as immovable as a setter at the scent of quail. His eyes were fixed upon Della, and there was an expression in them that she could not read, and it terrified her. It was not anger, nor surprise, nor disapproval, nor horror, nor any of the sentiments that she had been prepared for. He simply stared at her fixedly with that peculiar expression on his face.

Della wriggled off the table and went for him.

"Jim, darling," she cried, "don't look at me that way. I had my hair cut off and sold because

©Copyright 2006 by Barron's Educational Series, Inc.

GO ON →

I couldn't have lived through Christmas without giving you a present. It'll grow out again—you won't mind, will you? I just had to do it. My hair grows awfully fast. Say 'Merry Christmas!' Jim, and let's be happy. You don't know what a nice—what a beautiful, nice gift I've got for you."

"You've cut off your hair?" asked Jim, laboriously, as if he had not arrived at that patent fact yet even after the hardest mental labor.

"Cut it off and sold it," said Della. "Don't you like me just as well, anyhow? I'm me without my hair, ain't I?"

Jim looked about the room curiously.

"You say your hair is gone?" he said, with an air almost of idiocy.

"You needn't look for it," said Della. "It's sold, I tell you—sold and gone, too. It's Christmas Eve, boy. Be good to me, for it went for you. Maybe the hairs of my head were numbered," she went on with sudden serious sweetness, "but nobody could ever count my love for you. Shall I put the chops on, Jim?"

Out of his trance Jim seemed quickly to wake. He enfolded his Della. For ten seconds let us regard with discreet scrutiny some inconsequential object in the other direction. Eight dollars a week or a million a year—what is the difference? A mathematician or a wit would give you the wrong answer. The magi brought valuable gifts, but that was not among them. This dark assertion will be illuminated later on.

Jim drew a package from his overcoat pocket and threw it upon the table.

"Don't make any mistake, Dell," he said, "about me. I don't think there's anything in the way of a haircut or a shave or a shampoo that could make me like my girl any less. But if you'll unwrap that package you may see why you had me going a while at first."

White fingers and nimble tore at the string and paper. And then an ecstatic scream of joy; and then, alas! a quick feminine change to hysterical tears and wails, necessitating the immediate employment of all the comforting powers of the lord of the flat.

For there lay The Combs—the set of combs, side and back, that Della had worshipped long in a Broadway window. Beautiful combs, pure tortoise shell, with jeweled rims—just the shade to wear in the beautiful vanished hair. They were expensive combs,

GO ON →

she knew, and her heart had simply craved and yearned over them without the least hope of possession. And now, they were hers, but the tresses that should have adorned the coveted adornments were gone.

But she hugged them to her bosom, and at length she was able to look up with dim eyes and a smile and say: "My hair grows so fast, Jim!"

And then Della leaped up like a little singed cat and cried, "Oh, oh!"

Jim had not yet seen his beautiful present. She held it out to him eagerly upon her open palm. The dull precious metal seemed to flash with a reflection of her bright and ardent spirit.

"Isn't it a dandy, Jim? I hunted all over town to find it. You'll have to look at the time a hundred times a day now. Give me your watch. I want to see how it looks on it."

Instead of obeying, Jim tumbled down on the couch and put his hands under the back of his head and smiled.

"Dell," said he, "let's put our Christmas presents away and keep 'em a while. They're too nice to use just at present. I sold the watch to get the money to buy your combs. And now suppose you put the chops on."

Base your answers to questions 17 through 27 on the short story excertp "The Gift of the Magi."

17. What is the author's purpose in writing this short story?
  F. to explain the different types of Christmas gifts people give
  G. to illustrate the true meaning of love
  H. to describe the first Christmas together for Jim and Della
  I. to give a brief history of Jim and Della's relationship

18. Read the following line from the story:

Jim stopped inside the door, as immovable as a setter at the scent of quail. His eyes were fixed upon Della, and there was an expression in them that she could not read, and it terrified her.

The expression "as immovable as a setter at the scent of quail" means
A. as fixed on the task as possible.
B. wild with excitement.
C. as quiet as he could be.
D. as light as a bird.

19. Read the following line from the story:

For ten seconds let us regard with discreet scrutiny some inconsequential object in the other direction.

The word "scrutiny" means
F. careless observation.
G. reckless abandon.
H. careful investigation.
I. quick inspection.

20. Della prided herself in her adornments because
A. she believed they are what made Jim look at her.
B. she believed they added to her beauty.
C. she believed she was pretty enough without them.
D. she felt they were all that made her pretty.

21. Why did Della scream when she opened her gift?
F. She was surprised that Jim had bought her the very gift that she had always wanted.
G. She was scared of the gift inside.
H. She was expressing her distaste for the gift from Jim.
I. She was horrified that Jim had bought her an expensive comb.

22. Jim and Della both wanted to
A. buy a gift that they agreed upon together.
B. refrain from getting each other Christmas gifts that year.
C. surprise the other with a special Christmas gift.
D. buy a gift for their parents.

GO ON →

23. Which word best describes
BOTH Jim and Della?
F. selfish
G. uncooperative
H. lazy
I. self-sacrificing

24. Jim did not put his watch on at
the end of the story because
A. he had sold it to buy Della's
gift.
B. it didn't fit.
C. he had given it away.
D. he felt guilty because he
hadn't bought a gift for
Della.

25. What image from the beginning
of the story is repeated at the
end? Why?
F. The image of Jim smiling is
repeated because it shows
how happy a person he
was.
G. The image of pork chops is
repeated because it shows
that they would continue to
live life just as they had
before.
H. The image of Della smiling
is repeated because it
evokes emotion in the
reader.
I. The image of pork chops is
repeated because it
illustrates how poor Jim
and Della were.

26. READ/THINK/
EXPLAIN: This short
story is full of irony.
Describe some of the
irony, using details
and information to
explain your answer.

27. READ/THINK/
EXPLAIN: What
moral does this short
story teach, and how
does the story teach it?
Use details and
information from the
story to explain your
answer.

©Copyright 2006 by Barron's Educational Series, Inc.

GO ON →

Read the African-American fable "The Flying Contest" before answering questions 28 through 33.

The Flying Contest

One day, as the birds of a certain place were talking, an argument arose as to who could fly the highest. The smaller birds became quiet, for no one else listened to them anyway. It was the larger birds who boasted and argued. It was decided to hold a flying contest, after a few weeks of training for all the birds who wished to participate.

The smaller birds did not think they had a chance, and did not bother to strengthen their wings. This was except for the wren, who was aware of how small and weak she was. She tried to think of how she could win through trickery, and finally hatched a plan.

On the day of the contest, almost all the birds were saying that the eagle would win. The eagle was a swift, strong bird who spent each day flying higher than most birds did. The wren heard what the others were saying, and decided to stay as close to the eagle as she could. The birds swooped into the air and toward the clouds. It was not long before some of them began to fall behind. The wren managed to keep near the eagle.

Soon the birds soared into a cloud. The wren was so small and light that the eagle never noticed when she softly landed on the eagle's back. As the two passed upwards through the cloud, the other birds saw what had happened and cheered for the wren. The eagle thought

©Copyright 2006, 2001 by Barron's Educational Series, Inc.

GO ON →

that they were cheering for him, and beat his wings more strongly to show off. As he rose higher and higher, he called to the others he was leaving behind, "Who is flying the highest?"

"I am," said a tiny voice from above and behind him.

The eagle was astonished. He flew higher and asked again, "Who is flying the highest?"

"I am," the wren answered again.

The eagle angrily flew higher and higher, calling out the same question and getting the same answer. At last he was too exhausted to fly any more. He began to glide downward to rest. Then the wren let go and flew even higher. The eagle had to admit that the wren had won.

Base your answers to questions 28 through 33 on the fable "The Flying Contest."

28. Read the following sentence from the story:

It was the larger birds who boasted and argued.

The word "boasted" means
A. bluffed.
B. believed.
C. blamed.
D. bragged.

29. Why was the eagle astonished when he heard the tiny voice?
F. He thought only smaller birds could fly higher than he could.
G. He was amazed that anyone could fly higher than he could.
H. He thought only larger birds could fly higher than he could.
I. He was surprised that no one was flying higher than he was.

30. Who really won the flying contest?
A. the wren
B. the eagle
C. the larger birds
D. the smaller birds

©Copyright 2006 by Barron's Educational Series, Inc.

GO ON →

31. Read the following sentence from the story:

She tried to think of how she could win through trickery, and finally hatched a plan.

The sentence uses what literary device?
F. a metaphor
G. a simile
H. a pun
I. an allusion

32. The eagle thought everyone was cheering for him because
A. he had already won the race.
B. he was in the lead.
C. he had lost the race.
D. was the fastest bird.

33. READ/THINK/ EXPLAIN: Which bird do you believe was smarter? Why? Use details and examples from the story to explain your answer.

GO ON →

Read the article "How the Teddy Bear Got Its Name" before answering questions 34 through 39.

How the Teddy Bear Got Its Name

The actual date that the first teddy bear was made varies dependant on which book you read, and on where you believe the first Teddy Bear to have been made, the United States or Germany. In some ways, both countries can take credit for the first Teddy Bear.

Morris and Rose Mitchom, owners of a Brooklyn candy store in 1902, take credit for creating the first Teddy Bear in the United States after the incident described below and after seeing Berryman's cartoon.

On the 14 November 1902, Theodore Roosevelt, the 26th President of the United States of America took time out for relaxation after some hard political bargaining over the disputed boundaries between the states of Mississippi and Louisiana. His hosts took him on a hunting trip to an area near Little Sunflower River in Mississippi. In an effort to please the President a bear cub was captured, stunned and tied to a tree to ensure that the President had an easy target and would go home with a trophy.

However this plan backfired because the President refused to shoot the defenseless cub and ordered it to be set free. The press who were covering Roosevelt's visit quickly heard of the incident and the Washington Star's political cartoonist Clifford Berryman drew this cartoon of the incident entitled

©Copyright 2006 by Barron's Educational Series, Inc.

GO ON →

"Drawing the line at Mississippi." The cartoon emphasizes the child-like helplessness of the cub and was designed to convey the political message that such an upstanding President as Roosevelt could not be persuaded to make decisions for the wrong reasons. The cartoon was printed in all the papers and Roosevelt's popularity soared as a result of his actions. For the rest of his political career Roosevelt's mascot was "Teddy's Bear," which Berryman continued to use in all his cartoons and which played a key part in the President's successful re-election campaign of 1905.

Mr. Mitchom used the cartoon as a guide to design a pattern of the bear cub he had seen in the cartoon. With his wife's help he quickly created a little bear and put it in his store's window along with a copy of the cartoon. He called the toy "Teddy's Bear." It became so popular that within a year of its creation, Mr. Mitchom closed the candy store and founded the Ideal Novelty and Toy Company, which was, at one time, the largest bear factory in the United States and remains one of the biggest toy companies in the world today.

Almost at the same time in Germany Richard Steiff went to the Stuttgart Zoo in search of an idea for a new toy. Among the animals he saw there was a troupe of performing bears, which gave him an idea. He envisioned a toy bear, which stood upright, and was jointed similar to the way in which dolls were made. Richard sketched the bears and gave the drawings to his aunt, Margarete Steiff, a renowned toy maker and designer. Margarete took her nephew's drawings and designed a jointed bear based on them.

The new jointed bear appeared for the first time at the Leipzig Toy Fair in 1903. At first, no one seemed interested in the jointed bear. Then, as the story goes, while Richard was packing up his stand at the end of the fair, an American buyer approached him, and upon seeing the bear, immediately ordered several thousand. This was the beginning of the Steiff teddy bears we now all know and love.

—*Copyright Teddy Bear UK 2000.*
All rights reserved.

GO ON →

Base your answers to questions 34 through 39 on the article "How the Teddy Bear Got Its Name."

34. What is the main idea of this article?
  F. The origination of the teddy bear has more than one story.
  G. Teddy bears were invented in more than one country.
  H. A U.S. president invented the modern-day teddy bear.
  I. Teddy bears are the same all over the world.

35. This article is what type of literature?
  A. science fiction
  B. fiction
  C. historical fiction
  D. nonfiction

36. What do the two designers, Steiff and Berryman, have in common?
  F. Both mass-produced the teddy bear.
  G. Neither liked the original teddy bear design.
  H. Both could be credited with inventing the teddy bear.
  I. Neither actually invented the teddy bear.

37. What is the author's purpose in writing this article?
  A. to explain the origin of the teddy bear
  B. to entertain the reader with a fictional account of teddy bears
  C. to convince the reader to purchase teddy bears
  D. to describe the process of making a teddy bear

38. This article is written in a way that would most likely appeal to
  F. general readers.
  G. teddy bear collectors.
  H. children.
  I. toy makers.

39. READ/THINK/ EXPLAIN: Compare and contrast the two different designers. Use details and examples from the story to explain your answer.

Read the article "Inventor of Frozen Foods—Clarence Birdseye" before answering questions 40 through 45.

Inventor of Frozen Foods– Clarence Birdseye

By Mary Bellis

When we crave fresh fruits and vegetables in the middle of winter, we can thank Clarence Birdseye for the next best thing. Clarence Birdseye invented, developed, and commercialized a method for quick-freezing food products in convenient packages and without altering the original taste. While Clarence Birdseye has become a household name, his process has evolved into a multi-billion dollar industry.

Clarence Birdseye was born in 1886 in Brooklyn, New York. A taxidermist by trade, but a chef at heart, Clarence Birdseye wished his family could have fresh food all year. After observing the people of the Arctic preserving fresh fish and meat in barrels of sea water quickly frozen by the arctic tempera-

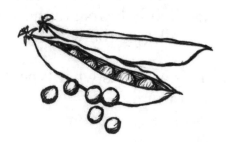

tures, he concluded that it was the rapid freezing in the extremely low temperatures that made food retain freshness when thawed and cooked months later.

In 1923, with an investment of $7 for an electric fan, buckets of brine, and cakes of ice, Clarence Birdseye invented and later perfected a system of packing fresh food into waxed cardboard boxes and flash freezing under high pressure. The Goldman-Sachs Trading Corporation and the Postum Company (later the General

GO ON →

Foods Corporation) bought Clarence Birdseye's patents and trademarks in 1929 for $22 million. The first quick-frozen vegetables, fruits, seafoods, and meat were sold to the public for the first time in 1930 in Springfield, Massachusetts, under the trade name Birds Eye Frosted Foods.

Clarence Birdseye turned his attention to other interests and invented an infrared heat lamp, a spotlight for store window displays, a harpoon for marking whales, then established companies to market his products.

Base your answers to questions 40 through 45 on the article "Inventor of Frozen Foods—Clarence Birdseye."

40. Read the following sentence from the article:

A taxidermist by trade, but a chef at heart, Clarence Birdseye wished his family could have fresh food all year.

What does "taxidermist" mean?
A. one who evades taxes
B. one who studies animals
C. one who prepares and stuffs the skins of animals
D. one who invents things

41. Which word best describes Clarence Birdseye?
F. resourceful
G. crafty
H. greedy
I. disinterested

42. READ/THINK/ EXPLAIN: How has Clarence Birdseye changed food storage? Use details and examples from the article to explain your answer.

43. The first quick-frozen food was sold in
A. the South.
B. the Northeast.
C. the Northwest.
D. Canada.

©Copyright 2006 by Barron's Educational Series, Inc.

GO ON →

44. Read the following sentence from the article:

In 1923, with an investment of $7 for an electric fan, buckets of brine, and cakes of ice, Clarence Birdseye invented and later perfected a system of packing fresh food into waxed cardboard boxes and flash freezing under high pressure.

The word "brine" means
F. salt
G. cold water
H. dry ice
I. preservative

45. How did Birdseye's experience and knowledge in other areas probably help him invent frozen food?
A. The concept of preservation in taxidermy influenced his desire to preserve food.
B. His time in the Arctic taught him how to freeze food properly.
C. His cooking talents helped him understand that food should be fresh.
D. All of the above.

This is the end of the FCAT Reading Test. Record the time in your answer booklet so that you can determine how long it took you to take this test. If it took you longer than the allowed 160 minutes, you should work on reading the passages and answering the questions more quickly.

FCAT WRITING+ TEST (ESSAY)

Writing Situation: *If you had to choose one season of the year as your favorite, which one would you chose?*

Directions for Writing: *Before you begin to write, think about the season you have chosen and why it is your favorite. You might be thinking about the weather, certain activities in this season, or both. Now write an essay in which you explain why this one season of the year is your favorite. Support your ideas with examples and details.*

This is the end of the Writing+ Test (Essay). Record the time in your answer booklet so that you can determine how long it took you to take this test. If it took you longer than the allowed 45 minutes, you should work on planning, writing, and proofreading/editing your essay more quickly.

©Copyright 2006 by Barron's Educational Series, Inc.

FCAT WRITING+ TEST (MULTIPLE CHOICE)

Stephen made the writing plan below to organize ideas for a paper he is writing. Read the writing plan and answer questions 1 through 3.

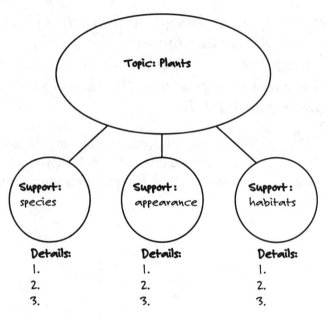

1. Under which subtopic should details about color, vines, and stalks be placed?
   A. species
   B. appearance
   C. habitats
   D. none of the above

2. Which detail below supports the subtopic "habitats"?
   F. desert, tundra, rain forest
   G. leafy, flowering, fruit-bearing
   H. green, yellow, brown
   I. all of the above

3. Based on his writing plan, what kind of paper is Stephen planning to write?
   A. a paper that explains the characteristics of plants
   B. a paper that compares two main types of plants
   C. a paper that describes the different types of plants
   D. a paper that persuades the reader to purchase plants

GO ON →

Jose made the outline below to organize ideas for a paper he is writing. Some of the details under the subtopics have not been listed yet. Read the writing plan and answer questions 4 through 6.

Racecar Driving

I. Famous drivers
II. Races
    A.
    B.
III. Tracks
    A.
    B.
IV. Sponsors

4. Which details should be listed under the fourth subtopic?
    F. Daytona International Speedway, Indianapolis Speedway, Atlanta Motor Speedway
    G. Daytona 500, Nextel Cup, Pepsi 400
    H. The Home Depot, DuPont, DeWalt Power Tools
    I. Dale Earnhart, Jr., Jeff Gordon, John Andretti

5. The subtopics of this formal outline indicate that the topic would be too
    A. short for a research paper.
    B. broad for an essay.
    C. vague for a personal letter.
    D. detailed for an editorial.

6. Under which subtopic should details about famous people be placed?
    F. drivers
    G. races
    H. tracks
    I. sponsors

©Copyright 2006 by Barron's Educational Series, Inc.

GO ON →

The essay below is a first draft that Devin wrote for his teacher. The essay contains errors. Read the essay and answer questions 7 through 12.

Golf

[1] Golf is a fun sport when you know what you're doing. [2] Besides the different types of clubs you can choose, there are different types of golf balls. [3] Also, knowing what types of courses there are helps you to prepare for the big game.

[4] Also there are different types of clubs. [5] The three types are oversized, normal, and blades. [6] The over sized irons are for below average, normal size for average, and blades for above average. [7] Name brands and styles may make a difference to some but not to the average golfer. [8] Some main brands are Taylor-made, Calaway, Clevland, Ping, and Titleist.

[9] There are many styles of golf balls such as Spin, Distance, control, and two piece. [10] Some major brands of golf balls are Nike, Titleist, Top-five, and Precept.

[11] There are two different types of courses, such as on restricted islands and cities there are chip and put courses which are made up of par threes and par fours. [12] The other type of course is the normal style which is made up of all different types of holes. [13] This is the type of course that you see more frequently. [14] Their are three options, you can ride in a cart or carry your bag but some courses have caddies to carry your bags for you.

[15] Golf is an interesting sport because it's simply knocking a little ball into a little cup with a stick. [16] Phil Mickelson is a great golfer. [17] In my opinion, golf is one of the most fun sports.

GO ON →

7. Which sentence contains a spelling error?
  A. sentence 2
  B. sentence 6
  C. sentence 10
  D. sentence 14

8. Which sentence should be deleted from paragraph 4 to maintain the focus?
  F. the first one
  G. the second one
  H. the third one
  I. the last one

9. Which sentence should be deleted because it presents a detail that is unrelated to the main points of the essay?
  A. sentence 4
  B. sentence 8
  C. sentence 10
  D. sentence 16

10. Which sentence below should Devin add to conclude his essay with a summary?
  F. Golf should be played by everyone.
  G. My favorite golfer is Tiger Woods.
  H. I would play golf every day if I could.
  I. The game of golf requires some basic knowledge of clubs, balls, and courses.

11. Devin wants to add the sentence below to his article:

  Golf balls on the other hand seem to go up in value and in price.

  Where should this sentence be added to keep the details in the correct order?
  A. at the beginning of paragraph 3
  B. at the beginning of paragraph 4
  C. at the end of paragraph 4
  D. at the beginning of paragraph 5

12. Why does Devin organize his essay the way he does?
  F. He wants to convince the reader to play golf.
  G. He wants to explain three major aspects of playing golf.
  H. He wants to list why golf is so difficult to play.
  I. He wants to explain why golf is so easy and fun to play.

GO ON →

The essay below is a first draft that Tonya wrote for her teacher. The essay contains errors. Read the essay and answer questions 13 through 18.

[1] Moving can be very fun. [2] You get a new house and new surrondings. [3] Moving can also be difficult. [4] You must do a lot of packing and unpacking. [5] Another part of moving that can be hard, or fun, is decorating.

[6] This can be very challenging. [7] You can buy a house. [8] That can take time, selecting the house you want to live in you can also choose to build a house. [9] This can take awhile because you have to select a lot, or somewhere to put your house. [10] Then you must wait for the builders to build your house. [11] Another choice you can make, is renting a house. [12] When renting a house, you need to find out if the house is worth how much the owner is renting it for.

[13] Next, you need to pack. [14] Packing can sometimes take days. [15] Things can also get broken if you're not careful. [16] Then, you have to put all your stuff in the moving van. [17] After you've arrived at your new house, you must unpack all of your belongings. [18] You might want to hire an interior decorator for your house when you're finished.

[19] Another thing you need to do when moving is decorate. [20] You need to choose paint or wallpaper for each room. [21] Then, you need to apply the paint or wallpaper. [22] Then, if your house does not have carpets, or if you do not like the carpets you have, you need to select a new carpet. [23] Then you need to lay it down. [24] Lastly, any other things like funiture or decorations need to be set up or bought.

[25] So, moving can be hard, like when you're packing. [26] Moving can be fun, when you decorate. [27] Moving is also costly, like when you're selecting a new house. [28] But, even if it is hard work, it will be worth it to have a new home that you like.

GO ON →

13. Which sentence below matches the tone of Tonya's essay?

A. There are more fun parts of moving than there are hard parts.

B. The difficulty of moving an entire household changes the dynamics of your family.

C. The stuff about moving that's cool is everything.

D. The pleasure of changing households brings enjoyment to the entire family.

14. Which revision below improves the following sentence by removing the spelling error?

Lastly, any other things like funiture or decorations need to be set up or bought.

F. Lastly, any other things like furniture or decorations need to be set up or baught.

G. Lastly, any other things like funiture or decorations need to be set up or baught.

H. Lastly, any other things like furniture or decorations need to be set up or bought.

I. Lastly, any other things like funiture or decorations need to be sat up or bought.

15. Which sentence below should be deleted from paragraph 3?

A. Packing can sometimes take days.

B. Things can also get broken if you're not careful.

C. Then, you have to put all your stuff in the moving van. After you've arrived at your new house, you must unpack all of your belongings.

D. You might want to hire an interior decorator for your house when you're finished.

16. Tonya wants to add the sentence below to her essay:

That can be a long, messy job.

After which sentence should this sentence be added to keep the details in the correct order?

F. sentence 1

G. sentence 9

H. sentence16

I. sentence 21

©Copyright 2006 by Barron's Educational Series, Inc.

GO ON →

17. Which transitional sentence should be added at the beginning of the second paragraph to show the connection between ideas in the essay?

A. My second reason for thinking moving is fun is that you get a new house.

B. When you move, you first need a new house.

C. First of all, packing can be difficult.

D. Lastly, you need a new house.

18. Read the following sentence from Tonya's essay:

Then, if your house does not have carpets, or if you do not like the carpets you have, you need to select a new carpet.

Which revision below improves this sentence by correcting the punctuation?

F. If your house does not have carpets, or if you do not like the carpets you have; you need to select a new carpet.

G. If your house does not have carpets or if you do not like the carpets you have, you need to select a new carpet.

H. If your house does not have carpets, or if you do not like the carpets you have, you need to select a new carpet.

I. If your house does not have carpets, or if you do not like the carpets you have you need to select a new carpet.

GO ON →

The essay below is a first draft that Jonathan wrote for his teacher. The essay contains errors. Read the essay and answer questions 19 through 24.

[1] When we heard my best friend from Atlanta was coming for a week we wanted show him a good time so we went to Orlando and went to two theme parks Blizzard Beach and Islands of Adventure. [2] He and I both were so excited; that's all we thought about!

[3] At Blizzard Beach they had the best waterslides! [4] The tallest and fastest water slide in the US called Summit Plummit was awesome. [5] But when the jets slowed u down near the bottom it was painful! [6] We still did it multiple times. [7] My friend Rob loved it. [8] Another great slide there was team boat springs where maximum of six people ride in one Raft and hit sharp turns and go fast. [9] It is one of the better rides at Blizzard Beach! [10] Blizzard Beach also had a wave pool! [11] It was pretty deep but the waves were so small.

[12] After Blizzard Beach we were on our way to the Portofino Bay Hotel inside Islands of Adventure! [13] My friend Rob and I got lost twice in the hotel. [14] It has a great location near Islands of

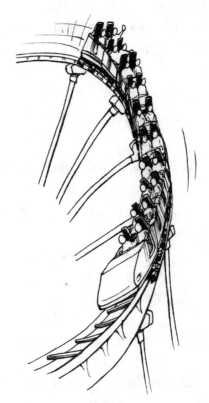

Adventure. [15] It is very nice; looking like a Italian town. [16] It got rated 5 stars, but I thought it was one of the worst hotels! [17] To get to your room you must go up three elevators. [18] The one benefit that made me choose this hotel was that the key card was an express pass meaning you could cut lines!

[19] We were off to Islands of Adventure. [20] First we wanted to do all the roller coasters so we did. [21] The incredible Hulk is awesome they shoot you out

at sixty miles per hour. [22] The dueling dragons were sweeeet! [23] We rode in the front row of both and it looks like there going to hit. [24] Fire and Ice are almost identical. [25] I preferred the Ice though. [26] Islands of Adventure also has the best food.

[27] In conclusion we had an awesome time even though it rained on us both days. [28] The Express Passes aloud us to ride too or three times more rides then normal.

19. Which sentence should be deleted because it presents a detail that is unimportant to the essay?
   A. the last sentence of paragraph 4
   B. the first sentence of paragraph 4
   C. the last sentence of paragraph 1
   D. the first sentence of paragraph 2

20. Read the following sentence from Jonathan's essay.

   The incredible Hulk is awesome they shoot you out at sixty miles per hour.

   Which revision below improves the sentence by correcting the errors?
   F. The incredible hulk is awesome, they shoot you out at sixty miles per hour.
   G. The Incredible Hulk is awesome; it shoots you out at sixty miles per hour.
   H. The Incredible Hulk is awesome they shoot you out at sixty miles per hour.
   I. The incredible Hulk is awesome: it shoots you out at sixty miles per hour.

GO ON →

21. Read the following sentence from Jonathan's essay:

The Express Passes aloud us to ride too or three times more rides then normal.

Which revision below improves the sentence by correcting the spelling error(s)?

A. The Express Passes allowed us to ride two or three times more rides than normal.

B. The Express Passes aloud us to ride too or three times more rides than normal.

C. The Express Passes aloud us to ride two or three times more rides than normal.

D. The Express Passes allowed us two ride two or three times more rides then normal.

22. Which transition should be added at the beginning of paragraph 4 to show the connection between ideas in the essay?

F. Finally

G. Before

H. The next morning

I. When

23. Read the following sentence from Jonathan's essay:

When we heard my best friend from Atlanta was coming for a week we wanted show him a good time so we went to Orlando and went to two theme parks Blizzard Beach and Islands of Adventure.

Which revision below improves this sentence by correcting the sentence structure and repetition?

A. When we heard my best friend from Atlanta was coming for a week, we wanted show him a good time by taking him to Blizzard Beach and Islands of Adventure in Orlando. So we went to Orlando and went to two theme parks.

B. When we heard my best friend from Atlanta was coming for a week, we wanted show him a good time, so we went to Orlando, and went to two theme parks, Blizzard Beach, and Islands of Adventure.

GO ON →

C. When we heard my best friend from Atlanta was coming for a week we wanted show him a good time; so we went to Orlando and went to two theme parks Blizzard Beach and Islands of Adventure.

D. When we heard my best friend from Atlanta was coming for a week, we wanted show him a good time by taking him to Blizzard Beach and Islands of Adventure in Orlando.

24. Which sentence below should be added to conclude the essay?

F. Our hotel was the best one in all of Orlando.

G. I would never go to Islands of Adventure again.

H. I would definitely go to Islands of Adventure again.

I. I always have fun with my best friend on trips.

GO ON →

The announcement below is a first draft that Abby wrote for her school's Physical Education (PE) department. The announcement contains errors. Read the announcement and answer questions 25 through 30.

Attention Future Cheerleaders:

[1] Tryouts for the ninth grade junior varsity cheerleading squad will be held next week after school in the gym from Tuesday until Thursday. [2] The squad members will be announced Friday morning on the morning news. [3] To try out, students must be in eighth grade this year. [4] Students in the sixth and seventh grades are not allowed to try out. [5] Based on enthusiasm, athletic skill, and precision, the JV cheerleading coach will decide which students will make the JV squad.

[6] All students interested must pick up papers from one of the PE coaches by Friday afternoon and return it complete by Monday morning. [7] Without a completed packet, including a signed parental permission form, students will not be permitted to try out. [8] Students must be prepared to attend each day's

tryouts. [9] It is important that students do not miss any days of tryouts.

Tuesday

[10] Each student trying out will be asked to perform an original 2–3 minute cheer routine. [11] Twenty students will be chosen to return the following day to learn a short JV cheer routine.

©Copyright 2006 by Barron's Educational Series, Inc.

GO ON →

Wednesday

[12] Next, the 20 selected students will meet to learn two new JV cheer routines. [13] This practice will begin promptly at 3:10 P.M. [14] Please dress apropriately with comfortable shoes.

Thursday

[15] All 20 students will be given an opportunity to perform the new routine as a group and individually for the final try out session. [16] This will probably last 2–3 hours. [17] Only 10 students (6 girls, 4 boys) will be selected for the JV squad and announced on Friday morning.

25. Which sentence contains an unimportant detail that should be deleted from the announcement?
    A. sentence 1
    B. sentence 2
    C. sentence 3
    D. sentence 4

26. Which sentence states information already presented and should be deleted from the announcement?
    F. sentence 9
    G. sentence 8
    H. sentence 7
    I. sentence 6

27. Which transition should be added at the beginning of sentence 10 to show the connection between ideas in the announcement?
    A. First
    B. Second
    C. Third
    D. Last

28. Which sentence below provides a necessary detail that supports sentence 10?
    F. Those who do not cheer well will not advance.
    G. Everyone will watch your routine.
    H. Wearing a cool outfit might help your chances of being selected.
    I. No music will be allowed to accompany the routine.

GO ON →

29. Read the following sentence from the announcement:

All students interested must pick up papers from one of the PE coaches by Friday afternoon and return it complete by Monday morning.

Which word(s) should replace "papers" in sentence 6 to make the wording more specific?
A. forms
B. an application packet
C. a packet of papers
D. a bunch of forms

30. Read the following sentence from Abby's announcement:

Please dress apropriately with comfortable shoes.

Which revision below improves the sentence by correcting the spelling error?
F. Please dress apropriatly with comfortable shoes.
G. Please dress apropriately with comforteable shoes.
H. Please dress appropriately with comfortable shoes.
I. Please dress appropriatly with comfortable shoes.

©Copyright 2006 by Barron's Educational Series, Inc.

GO ON →

Read the article "Florida's Black Bears: Abundant or Endanged?" and answer questions 31 through 36.

Florida's Black Bears: Abundant, or Endangered?

By Kristen Sternberg, Newspaper In Education Educational Consultant

Nobody really knows how many Florida black bears (31)_____. Over the years, people have cleared forests for space to live and work, and to sell the lumber and other products from the trees. As a result, there are a lot fewer bears than there once were. Bears require a lot of space to roam and forage for food, and (32) _____ are constantly on the move, so it's hard to get an accurate count. Scientists estimate, however, that between 1,200 and 1,800 Florida black bears are currently living.

Therefore, the bears are labeled as a threatened species. Whether their numbers increase, or whether they become more endangered, depends on many factors, such as loss of habitat, (33)_____ conditions and human interference.

Due to efforts by conservationists, there are signs that the bear population is on the rise. A large number of black bears live in the Ocala National Forest. There, the (34) _____ numbers are increasing. However, with the human population of (35) _____ also growing, problems are bound to occur.

GO ON →

Bears frequently wander into areas where people live. As more and more forests are cleared for development and industry, new roads are built to provide access, and when a bear and a car collide, the bear usually loses.

Reports of bears killed on Florida roads (36) _____ more and more common.

—http://www.nieworld.com/special/hotcold/2001/blckbear.htm

Choose the word or words that correctly complete questions 31 through 36 and mark your answers on the Sample Answer Sheet.

31. Which answer should go in blank 31?
  A. they're
  B. there are
  C. their are

32. Which answer should go in blank 32?
  F. he
  G. it
  H. they

33. Which answer should go in blank 33?
  A. drought
  B. draught
  C. drowt

34. Which answer should go in blank 34?
  F. bear's
  G. bears'
  H. bears's

35. Which answer should go in blank 35?
  A. Central Florida
  B. central Florida
  C. Central florida

36. Which answer should go in blank 36?
  F. became
  G. is becoming
  H. are becoming

©Copyright 2006 by Barron's Educational Series, Inc.

GO ON →

Read the questions below; answer questions 37 through 45 on your Sample Answer Sheet.

37. In which sentence below is all the capitalization correct?
  A. LaTesha lives at 123 Magnolia Avenue.
  B. laTesha lives at 123 magnolia avenue.
  C. laTesha lives at 123 Magnolia avenue.

38. In which sentence below is the sentence structure effective?
  F. Too tired to wake up, Jillian threw her alarm clock across the room.
  G. Too tired to wake up, Jillian's alarm clock was thrown across the room.
  H. Too tired to wake up, Jillian's mom had to get her out of bed.

39. In which sentence below are all the grammar and usage correct?
  A. The students were asked to put his and her backpacks away.
  B. The students were asked to put his backpacks away.
  C. The students were asked to put their backpacks away.

40. In which sentence below is all the spelling correct?
  F. When the teacher collected their homework, there were five papers missing.
  G. When the teacher collected there homework, their were five papers missing.
  H. When the teacher collected there homework, they're were five papers missing.

41. In which sentence below are all the grammar and usage correct?
  A. Each of the students are keeping a writing notebook for the entire year in Language Arts.
  B. Each of the students has a writing notebook for the entire year in Language Arts.
  C. Each of the students have a writing notebook for the entire year in Language Arts.

GO ON →

42. In which sentence below is all the punctuation correct?

F. The trip to the Holocaust Museum in Washington DC lasted only a few hours, however, it left an impression on the students for a long time.

G. The trip to the Holocaust Museum in Washington DC lasted only a few hours; however, it left an impression on the students for a long time.

H. The trip to the Holocaust Museum in Washington DC lasted only a few hours: however, it left an impression on the students for a long time.

43. In which sentence below is all the punctuation correct?

A. Having a hobby keeps Jose content, but his mom has to work longer hours so she has enough money for his supplies.

B. Having a hobby keeps Jose content but his mom has to work longer hours so she has enough money for his supplies.

C. Having a hobby keeps Jose content; but his mom has to work longer hours so she has enough money for his supplies.

44. In which sentence below is all the spelling correct?

F. Dogs are so much cuter when they are puppies.

G. Dogs are so much cuter when they are puppys.

H. Dogs are so much cuter when they are puppees.

©Copyright 2006 by Barron's Educational Series, Inc.

GO ON →

45. In which sentence below are all the grammar and usage correct?

   A. Being the only redhead and the only boy, Jimmy stood out on stage when the choir sang.

   B. Being the only redhead and a boy, Jimmy stood out on stage when the choir sang.

   C. Being the only redhead and being the only boy, Jimmy stood out on stage when the choir sang.

This is the end of the Writing+ Test (Multiple Choice). Record the time in your answer booklet so that you can determine how long it took you to take this test. If it took you longer than the allowed 90 minutes, you should work on reading the passages and answering the questions more quickly.

FCAT READING TEST ANSWERS AND EXPLANATIONS

Note to students:
As you read through the correct answers, pay close attention to the explanations of the answers. The Florida Sunshine State Standards listed as benchmarks for each question tell you what type of skill is being tested in the question. (A complete list of the benchmarks associated with the Sunshine State Standards can be found in the Appendix.)

Note to parents and teachers:
Pay close attention to the benchmarks listed. They indicate the type of skill being tested in each particular question according to the Florida Sunshine State Standards. Use these skills to provide similar practice before the test. (A complete list of the benchmarks associated with the Sunshine State Standards can be found in the Appendix.)

1. The correct answer is B (only for the past 100 years).

Type of passage: Informational text

Benchmark: LA.A.1.3.2

The correct answer is B. The first paragraph in the article, specifically the first sentence, clearly states, "Scientists have only been studying hurricanes for about 100 years." Even though evidence has been found dating back thousands of years, scientists have only been studying this evidence for 100 years.

2. The correct answer is I (a destructive force over the history of humanity).

Type of passage: Informational text

Benchmark: LA.A.2.3.1

The correct answer is I. The author describes all the ways that hurricanes have destroyed civilizations and fleets of ships over the years. Everything in the article supports the statement that hurricanes have been a destructive force throughout history.

©Copyright 2006 by Barron's Educational Series, Inc.

3. The correct answer is C (many ships).

    Type of passage: Informational text

    Benchmark: LA.A.1.3.2

    The correct answer is C. Of the available options, only "many ships" makes sense in the sentence. The clue is in the first part of the sentence, which reads, "Some of the ships were damaged. . . ." Therefore, many ships make up a fleet.

4. The correct answer is F (to give a brief history of hurricanes).

    Type of passage: Informational text

    Benchmark: L.A.A.2.2.2

    The correct answer is F. In every paragraph, the author gives information about what damage hurricanes have done, the origin of the name for hurricanes, and what specific hurricanes have done over the years. In just five paragraphs, a brief overview of hurricanes is presented.

5. The correct answer is C (131 to 155 mph).

    Type of passage: Informational text

    Benchmark: LA.A.2.3.5

    The correct answer is C. In the article, the famous storm is described as a Category 4. According to the Saffir-Simpson Scale, a Category 4 hurricane has winds of 131 to 155 mph.

6. The correct answer is F (Category 1 hurricanes do less damage than Category 5 hurricanes).

    Type of passage: Informational text

    Benchmark: LA.A.2.3.5

    The correct answer is F. On the scale, Category 5 hurricanes do the worst damage because they destroy roofs, cause flooding, and require people to be evacuated. Category 1 hurricanes do not result in this type of damage, only minor flooding.

7. Use the extended-response scoring rubric in Chapter 5 to score this response (4-point scoring rubric).

Type of passage: Informational text

Benchmark: LA.A.2.2.1

A top-score response would include examples of damage hurricanes have done to civilizations over time. The response would be supported with details and information from the article for example:

Over time, hurricanes have been known to destroy fleets of ships, as well as whole areas of civilizations. There is a lot of evidence that hurricanes have been affecting our land and people for thousands of years. Scientists even believe that parts of a lake in Alabama got there from a hurricane that occurred as many as 3,000 years ago.

The article states, "Many storms left important marks on history." One example is the island of Bermuda that was actually founded by people who were stranded after a hurricane. Without that hurricane to destroy their ship and leave them stranded, the island may not have been discovered for many, many

years. Also, there is evidence of severe hurricanes that have hit America, killing many people in states like Louisiana, South Carolina, Texas, and Georgia.

8. The correct answer is B (above).

Type of passage: Literary text

Benchmark: LA.A.1.3.2

The correct answer is B. In the context of the sentence, Revere's friend was to hang his lantern high in the air so that he (Revere) could see it from below. Therefore, "aloft" means "above."

9. The correct answer is H (The men and women buried in the cemetery).

Type of passage: Literary text

Benchmark: LA.A.1.3.2

The correct answer is H. The people who "lay dead" in the churchyard are men and women buried in a cemetery. Most cemeteries were located next to churches. Although the passage indicates the people were "encamped on the hill," it does not mean they were soldiers who were killed there. The British hadn't even landed yet, so they could not have been killed by them.

©Copyright 2006 by Barron's Educational Series, Inc.

10. The correct answer is C (to inform the reader of the famous midnight ride of Paul Revere by entertaining).

Type of Passage: Literary text

Benchmark: LA.A.2.3.2

The correct answer is C. The poem is an entertaining historical account of Paul Revere. The first stanza states this purpose clearly: "Listen my children and you shall hear/Of the midnight ride of Paul Revere,/On the eighteenth of April, in Seventy-five;/Hardly a man is now alive/Who remembers that famous day and year."

11. The correct answer is I (to alarm the people that the British are coming).

Type of passage: Literary text

Benchmark: LA.E.2.3.1

The correct answer is I. The only choice that states Revere's main goal is "To alarm the people that the British are coming" because everything Revere does is to warn the people in time so that they can defend themselves. The first two choices are both actions Revere took in the poem, but not his overall goal.

12. The correct answer is D (He must warn his countrymen that the enemy has arrived during the night so that they are not killed in their sleep and lose the war).

Type of passage: Literary text

Benchmark: LA.E.2.3.1

The correct answer is D. If Revere doesn't act quickly, his countrymen may die. The British want to attack at night to catch the people off guard, but if Revere's countrymen are prepared, they can successfully defend themselves.

13. The correct answer is F (The British are Revere's enemy).

Type of passage: Literary text

Benchmark: LA.E.2.3.1

The correct answer is F. Because he is about to warn his countrymen that the British are coming and to "take arm," Revere believes the British to be his enemy. If they were not his enemy, he would not be concerned about this night operation. Also, he is anxious for them to arrive, but his actual attitude is that they are his enemy.

14. Use the short-response scoring rubric in Chapter 5 to score this response (2-point scoring rubric).

Type of passage: Literary text

Benchmark: LA.E.2.3.1

A top-score response would include the following information: "Trembling ladder" indicates that the person is shaking from fear or nervousness. "Paused to listen" indicates concentration. The response would be supported with details and information from the poem. For example:

The quotation shows that the mood of Revere's friend was one of nervousness because he was not only afraid of the approaching enemy, but he wanted to be sure to give the correct symbol to Revere. The "trembling ladder" shows that he was scared as he was climbing it to show the signal to Revere. Then, when the poem says that he "paused to listen," it reveals that his friend was trying to concentrate to make sure he would hear any noise of which direction the British were coming.

15. The correct answer is D (narrative).

Type of passage: Literary text

Benchmark: LA.A.2.2.2

The correct answer is D. The poem tells a story of a historical event, which makes it a narrative poem. It does not only persuade, inform, or explain the event.

16. Use the short-response scoring rubric in Chapter 5 to score this response (2-point scoring rubric).

Type of passage: Literary text

Benchmark: LA.E.1.3.4

A top-score response would include information about the patterns that rhythm and rhyme create in the poem. The response would be supported with details and information from the poem. For example:

In the poem, there is a rhyme scheme that helps the reader to follow the events easily. This pattern of similar sounds allows the reader to imagine the sounds that Revere might have heard while riding that famous night. The rhythm creates a "clickety-clack" sound, like that of the horse's hoofs on the road. With the combination of the rhyme scheme and rhythm, the reader feels as if he is riding along with Revere, making the poem a personal experience.

17. The correct answer is G (to illustrate the true meaning of love).

Type of passage: Literary text

Benchmark: LA.A.2.2.2

The correct answer is G. Jim and Della both want to buy a Christmas gift for the other that is very special.

18. The correct answer is A (as fixed on the task as possible).

Type of passage: Literary text

Benchmark: LA.A.1.3.2

The correct answer is A because, like a dog who would not leave the scent of a bird, Jim would not take his eyes off Della in anticipation of giving her the gift he had purchased.

19. The correct answer is H (careful investigation).

Type of passage: Literary text

Benchmark: LA.A.1.3.2.

The correct answer is H. The correct definition of the word is "careful investigation."

20. The correct answer is B (she believed they added to her beauty).

Type of passage: Literary text

Benchmark: LA.A.2.3.1

The correct answer is B. Della believed that her adornments simply added to her beauty because she knew that without her hair, Jim would still think she was beautiful.

21. The correct answer is F (She was surprised that Jim had bought her the very gift that she had always wanted).

Type of passage: Literary text

Benchmark: LA.A.2.3.1

The correct answer is F. Della didn't expect to get the combs for Christmas, so she didn't even think that by selling her hair she wouldn't be able to use the gift Jim was about to give her.

22. The correct answer is C (surprise the other with a special Christmas gift).

Type of passage: Literary text

Benchmark: LA.A.2.3.1

The correct answer is C. They each wanted to get a buy that the other wasn't expecting.

23. The correct answer is I (self-sacrificing).

Type of passage: Literary text

Benchmark: LA.A.2.3.1

The correct answer is I. Both Della and Jim each gave up something very special in order to get a gift the other would treasure.

24. The correct answer is A (he had sold it to buy Della's gift).

Type of passage: Literary text

Benchmark: LA.A.2.3.1

The correct answer is A. Jim no longer had the watch because he had sold it in order to get enough money to buy Della a gift. He couldn't put on a watch that he didn't have.

25. The correct answer is G (The image of pork chops is repeated because it shows that they would continue to live life just as they had before).

Type of passage: Literary text

Benchmark: LA.A.2.3.1

The correct answer is G. The first sentence reads, "At 7 o'clock the coffee was made and the frying pan was on the back of the stove hot and ready to cook the chops." Jim is mentioned to be cooking the pork chops in the beginning and again at the end of the story. This image portrays Jim and Della as doing everyday things at the end of the story, as if life would continue as before.

26. Use the short-response scoring rubric in Chapter 5 to score this response (2-point scoring rubric).

Type of passage: Literary text

Benchmark: LA.E.1.3.3

A top-score response would include examples of irony. For example:

The main examples of irony are the gifts that Jim and Della bought for each other. Jim's most prized possession was a pocket watch. That's why Della sold her long, beautiful locks for enough money to buy Jim a nice chain to attach to his watch. However, Jim had sold his watch in order to buy beautiful hair combs for Della. These gifts end up to be ironic because neither one could use the gift and each had given up something special for the other.

©Copyright 2006 by Barron's Educational Series, Inc.

27. Use the extended-response scoring rubric in Chapter 5 to score this response (4-point scoring rubric).

Type of passage: Literary text

Benchmark: LA.E.1.3.3

A top-score response would include the moral of this story and how it is taught to the reader. For example:

The moral of this story is to sacrifice for those you love. The title of the short story is "The Gift of the Magi," which refers to the gifts that were brought to Jesus in Bethlehem. They were expensive gifts that must have cost the kings (magi) a lot. However, giving a gift that is a sacrifice means more. I believe the author wants the reader to think more of others than himself.

28. The correct answer is D (bragged).

Type of passage: Literary text

Benchmark: LA.A.1.3.2

The correct answer is D. A synonym for the phrase "to boast" is "to brag."

29. The correct answer is G (He was amazed that anyone could fly higher than he could).

Type of passage: Literary text

Benchmark: LA.A.1.3.2

The correct answer is G. The eagle did not believe any bird could fly higher than he could, so he was surprised to hear a voice answer him.

30. The correct answer is A (the wren).

Type of Passage: Literary text

Benchmark: LA.E.2.3.1

The correct answer is A. Because the wren stayed on the back of the eagle, she was always flying higher than the eagle, which means she won the contest.

31. The correct answer is H (a pun).

Type of passage: Literary text

Benchmark: LA.E. 1.3.4.

The correct answer is H. Instead of saying that the wren came up with a plan, the author created a pun by saying the wren "hatched a plan." Normally, birds hatch only eggs!

32. The correct answer is B (he was in the lead).

Type of passage: Literary text

Benchmark: LA.E.1.3.2

The correct answer is B. The eagle was arrogant and believed he was winning, yet he didn't realize that he was being outsmarted.

33. Use the short-response scoring rubric in Chapter 5 to score this response (2-point scoring rubric).

Type of passage: Literary text

Benchmark: LA.E.1.3.2

A top-score response would include the following information: which bird was smarter and concrete examples to support the position. In defense of the wren, examples of how the wren used her mind to defeat her competition. For example:

Obviously, the wren was smarter. I say this because I don't think the wren was trying to use trickery to win, but instead used her mental abilities. All of the other birds, including the eagle, were trying to win this contest by using their physical strength. The wren looked at the competition, knowing that she could not out-fly an eagle, the

most powerful bird in the world, and instead prepared mentally for the challenge. There were no rules against what the wren did.

34. The correct answer is F (The origination of the teddy bear has more than one story).

Type of passage: Informative text

Benchmark: LA.A.2.3.1

The correct answer is F. The story actually explains two origins of the modern-day teddy bear.

35. The correct answer is D (nonfiction).

Type of passage: Informative text

Benchmark: LA.E.2.3.2

The correct answer is D. Although the origins are stories, each is told as people believe them to be. The story is not completely made up.

36. The correct answer is H (Both could be credited with inventing the teddy bear).

Type of passage: Informative text

Benchmark: LA.A.2.2.7

The correct answer is H. Both stories describe valid originations of the teddy bear.

©Copyright 2006 by Barron's Educational Series, Inc.

37. The correct answer is A (to explain the origin of the teddy bear).

Type of passage: Informative text

Benchmark: LA.A.2.2.2

The correct answer is A. The author simply wanted to explain where and how the teddy bear was invented.

38. The correct answer is F (general readers).

Type of passage: Informative text

Benchmark: LA.E.2.3.3.

The correct answer is F. General readers would be interested in this story, not just collectors, children, and/or toymakers.

39. Use the Short-Response scoring rubric in Chapter 5 to score this response (2-point scoring rubric).

Type of passage: Informative text

Benchmark: LA.A.2.2.7

A top-score response would include the following information: similarities and differences between the two designers. For example:

Morris and Rose Mitchom are believed to have made the first teddy bear in the United States. They patterned their model on a cartoon that was created after Theodore Roosevelt went hunting and refused to shoot a bear cub. While at the same time, Richard Steiff from Germany was in search of a new idea for a toy. He came up with his idea by going to the Stuttgart Zoo. His aunt ended up making the bear for him. This toy appeared at the Leipzig Toy Fair where someone saw the bear and bought many of them. Both designers came up with the idea for a toy bear, but one was in the US and capitalized on the President's association with the bear. The other wanted to create a new toy and came up with the same idea. They both created the teddy bear around the same time and were both very successful.

40. The correct answer is C (one who prepares and stuffs the skins of animals).

Type of passage: Informative text

Benchmark: LA.A.1.3.2

The correct answer is C because it gives the correct definition of "taxidermist."

41. The correct answer is F (resourceful).

Type of passage: Informative text

Benchmark: LA.A.1.3.2

The correct answer is F. Birdseye used the resources he had to invent a system for freezing food.

42. Use the extended-response scoring rubric in Chapter 5 to score this response (4-point scoring rubric).

Type of passage: Informative text

Benchmark: LA.E.2.3.2

A top-score response would include the following information: many of the changes since frozen foods were invented, such as changed food storage, freezers, popsicles, TV dinners, and so on. For example:

Clarence Birdseye has greatly changed food storage. Before frozen foods, people had to make all of their meals. Food preparation took longer, too. But since frozen foods were available to everyone in the grocery stores, people could buy frozen meals that could easily be heated, saving a lot of time for the person cooking the meal. Also, storage containers had to be invented to contain the frozen foods. More people bought freezers. And other foods were made available, such as popsicles and TV dinners.

43. The correct answer is B (the Northeast).

Type of passage: Informative text

Benchmark: LA.A.1.3.2

The correct answer is B. The first quick-frozen food was sold in Springfield, Massachussetts, which is in the Northeast.

44. The correct answer is F (salt).

Type of passage: Informative text

Benchmark: LA.A.1.3.2

The correct answer is F. Brine comes from seawater, which contains salt.

45. The correct answer is D (all of the above).

Type of passage: Informative text

Benchmark: LA.A.1.3.2.

The correct answer is D. All of Birdseye's experience helped him to invent his method of flash-freezing.

©Copyright 2006 by Barron's Educational Series, Inc.

FCAT WRITING+ TEST ANSWERS AND EXPLANATIONS

Note to students:
As you read through the correct answers, pay close attention to the explanations of the answers. The Florida Sunshine State Standards listed as benchmarks for each question tell you what type of skill is being tested in the question. (A complete list of the benchmarks associated with the Sunshine State Standards can be found in the Appendix.)

Note to parents and teachers:
Pay close attention to the benchmarks listed. The indicate the type of skill being tested in each particular question according to the Florida Sunshine State Standards. Use these skills to provide similar practice before the test. (A complete list of the benchmarks associated with the Sunshine State Standards can be found in the Appendix.)

1. The correct answer is B (appearance).

   Item type: Stimulus-based

   Category: Focus

   Benchmark: LA.B.1.3.1.

   The correct answer is B. Details about color, vines, and stalks should be placed under the subtopic "appearance."

2. The correct answer is F (desert, tundra, rain forest).

   Item type: Stimulus-based

   Category: Focus

   Benchmark: LA.B.1.3.1.

   The correct answer is F, because these are different types of habitats where plants can grow.

3. The correct answer is A (a paper that explains the characteristics of plants).

   Item type: Stimulus-based

   Category: Focus

   Benchmark: LA.B.1.3.1.

   The correct answer is A, because the subtopics listed (species, appearance, habitats) are all characteristics describing plants.

4. The correct answer is H (The Home Depot, DuPont, DeWalt Power Tools).

Item type: Stimulus-based

Category: Focus

Benchmark: LA.B.1.3.1.

The correct answer is H, because these are all names of companies that sponsor racecars.

5. The correct answer is B (broad for an essay).

Item type: Stimulus-based

Category: Focus

Benchmark: LA.B.1.3.1.

The correct answer is B because the subtopics could not be completely elaborated in just one paragraph each.

6. The correct answer is F (drivers).

Item type: Stimulus-based

Category: Organization

Benchmark: LA.B.1.3.1

The correct answer is F because people are drivers.

7. The correct answer is D (sentence 14).

Item type: Sample-based

Category: Support

Benchmark: LA.B.1.3.2.

The correct answer is D because "Their" should be written "There." "Their" means "belongs to them," whereas "There" is paired with the linking verb "are" to indicate where something or someone is located.

8. The correct answer is H (the last one).

Item type: Sample-based

Category: Focus

Benchmark: LA.B.1.3.2.

The correct answer is H because the last sentence talks about having caddies to carry your bags, whereas the rest of the paragraph is about the two different types of courses.

©Copyright 2006 by Barron's Educational Series, Inc.

9. The correct answer is D (sentence 16).

Item type: Sample-based

Category: Focus/organization/support

Benchmark: LA.B.1.3.2.

The correct answer is D. The sentence "Phil Mickelson is a great golfer" has nothing to do with the main idea of the essay, which is that golf is an interesting sport.

10. The correct answer is I (The game of golf requires some basic knowledge of clubs, balls, and courses).

Item type: Sample-based

Category: Focus/organization/support

Benchmark: LA.B.1.3.2.

The correct answer is I. This choice is the only one that summarizes the main idea of the essay, which is that "golf requires basic knowledge of clubs, balls, and courses."

11. The correct answer is A (at the beginning of paragraph 3).

Item type: Sample-based

Category: Focus/organization/support

Benchmark: LA.B.1.3.2.

The correct answer is A. Paragraph 3 talks about types of golf balls, so the sentence "Golf balls on the other hand seem to go up in value and in price" should be added to this paragraph.

12. The correct answer is G (He wants to explain three major aspects of playing golf).

Item type: Sample-based

Category: Focus/organization/support

Benchmark: LA.B.1.3.2.

The correct answer is G. From Devin's introductory paragraph, note that he is going to explain three major aspects of the game of golf.

13. The correct answer is A (There are more fun parts of moving than there are hard parts).

Item type: Sample-based

Category: Focus/organization/support

Benchmark: LA.B.1.3.2.

The correct answer is A. This choice uses the same language that Tonya uses in her essay. The other choices use a higher vocabulary except for one that uses a lesser vocabulary (choice C).

14. The correct answer is H (Lastly, any other things like furniture or decorations need to be set up or bought).

Item type: Sample-based

Category: Conventions

Benchmark: LA.B.1.3.3.

The correct answer is H. There is one spelling mistake to be corrected in this sentence: "furniture."

15. The correct answer is D (You might want to hire an interior decorator for your house when you're finished).

Item type: Sample-based

Category: Focus/organization/support

Benchmark: LA.B.1.3.2.

The correct answer is D. Paragraph 3 is about packing, so the sentence about hiring an interior decorator does not match the main idea.

16. The correct answer is I (sentence 21).

Item type: Sample-based.

Category: Support

Benchmark: LA.B.1.3.2.

The correct answer is I because the previous sentence describes applying paint or wallpaper, which can both be long and messy jobs.

17. The correct answer is B (When you move, you first need a new house).

Item type: Sample-based

Category: Focus/organization/support

Benchmark: LA.B.1.3.2.

The correct answer is B. The second paragraph talks about buying a house, so this sentence is a logical introductory sentence. It is also the first point in the essay, so using the transitional word "first" is important to indicate there will be other actions taken.

18. The correct answer is H (If your house does not have carpets, or if you do not like the carpets you have, you need to select a new carpet).

Item type: Sample-based

Category: Focus/organization/support

Benchmark: LA.B.1.3.2.

©Copyright 2006 by Barron's Educational Series, Inc.

The correct answer is H. There are two long introductory phrases in this sentence that must be set off by commas.

19. The correct answer is A (the last sentence of paragraph 4).

Item type: Sample-based

Reporting Category: Focus/organization/support

Benchmark: LA.B.1.3.2.

The correct answer is A. The sentence "Islands of Adventure also has the best food" does not have anything to do with the main idea of the paragraph, which is about riding roller coasters.

20. The correct answer is G (The Incredible Hulk is awesome; it shoots you out at sixty miles per hour).

Item type: Sample-based

Category: Focus/organization/support

Benchmark: LA.B.1.3.2.

The correct answer is G. This choice uses a semicolon to separate the two clauses and uses the correct pronoun "it" to replace "The Incredible Hulk."

21. The correct answer is A (The Express Passes allowed us to ride two or three times more rides than normal).

Item type: Sample-based

Category: Conventions

Benchmark: LA.B.1.3.3.

The correct answer is A. The two words misspelled are "allowed" and "two." This choice is the only one with both words spelled correctly.

22. The correct answer is F (Finally).

Item type: Sample-based

Category: Focus/organization/support

Benchmark: LA.B.1.3.2.

The correct answer is F. Because this is the last body paragraph, the transition "finally" is appropriate to show the ending of the main points.

23. The correct answer is D (When we heard my best friend from Atlanta was coming for a week, we wanted to show him a good time by taking him to Blizzard Beach and Islands of Adventure in Orlando).

Item type: Sample-based

Category: Focus/organization/support

Benchmark: LA.B.1.3.2.

The correct answer is D. This is the only choice that uses the introductory phrase with a comma before the main clause and uses the least amount of words to explain the point being made.

24. The correct answer is H (I would definitely go to Islands of Adventure again).

Item type: Sample-based

Category: Focus/organization/support

Benchmark: LA.B.1.3.2.

The correct answer is H. To conclude this essay, the choice is the only one that agrees with the main idea of the essay.

25. The correct answer is D (sentence 4).

Item type: Sample-based

Category: Focus/organization/support

Benchmark: LA.B.1.3.2.

The correct answer is D. Because the announcement already mentions that only

eighth graders are allowed to try out, it is not necessary to mention that sixth and seventh graders are not allowed to try out. That would be redundant.

26. The correct answer is F (sentence 9).

Item type: Sample-based

Category: Focus/organization/support

Benchmark: LA.B.1.3.2.

The correct answer is F. Sentence 9 restates that students must attend each day of tryouts. It is not necessary to repeat information.

27. The correct answer is A (First).

Item type: Sample-based

Category: Focus/organization/support

Benchmark: LA.B.1.3.2.

The correct answer is A. The transition "First" is necessary to show that Tuesday is the first day of tryouts.

28. The correct answer is I (No music will be allowed to accompany the routine).

Item type: Sample-based

Category: Focus/organization/support

Benchmark: LA.B.1.3.2.

The correct answer is I. Sentence 10 states, "Each student trying out will be asked to perform an original 2–3 minute cheer routine." The only choice that gives important information to those trying out is this one.

29. The correct answer is B (an application packet).

Item type: Sample-based

Category: Focus/organization/support

Benchmark: LA.B.1.3.2.

The correct answer is B. The papers necessary to try out are the application packet of papers. This is the only specific choice.

30. The correct answer is H (Please dress appropriately with comfortable shoes).

Item type: Sample-based

Category: Focus/organization/support

Benchmark: LA.B.1.3.2.

The correct answer is H. Two words are misspelled in the choices: "appropriately" and "comfortable." This choice is the only one with both spelled correctly.

31. The correct answer is B (there are)

Item type: Cloze-based

Category: Conventions

Benchmark: LA.B.1.3.3.

Benchmark clarification: The student will demonstrate knowledge of the conventions of correct spelling.

The correct answer is B; "there are" is the correct phrase to complete the sentence.

32. The correct answer is H (they).

Item type: Cloze-based

Category: Conventions

Benchmark: LA.B.1.3.3.

The correct answer is H; "they" is the correct choice because it is the plural pronoun replacing the noun "bears."

33. The correct answer is A (drought).

Item type: Cloze-based

Category: Conventions

Benchmark: LA.B.1.3.3.

The correct answer is A. This is the only choice with the word "drought" spelled correctly.

34. The correct answer is G (bears').

Item type: Cloze-based

Category: Conventions

Benchmark: LA.B.1.3.3.

The correct answer is G, because it shows that "bears'" is both plural and possessive.

35. The correct answer is A (Central Florida).

Item type: Cloze-based

Category: Conventions

Benchmark: LA.B.1.3.3.

The correct answer is A because both words in the proper noun must be capitalized.

36. The correct answer is H (are becoming).

Item type: Cloze-based

Category: Conventions

Benchmark: LA.B.1.3.3.

The correct answer is H because the subject, "reports," is plural.

37. The correct answer is A (LaTesha lives at 123 Magnolia Avenue).

Item type: Cloze-based

Category: Conventions

Benchmark: LA.B.1.3.3.

The correct answer is A because both proper nouns must be capitalized—LaTesha and Magnolia Avenue.

38. The correct answer is F (Too tired to wake up, Jillian threw her alarm clock across the room).

Item type: Cloze-based

Category: Conventions

Benchmark: LA.B.1.3.3.

The correct answer is F because it is the only one that matches the beginning modifier "too tired to wake up."

39. The correct answer is C (The students were asked to put their backpacks away).

Item type: Cloze-based

Category: Conventions

Benchmark: LA.B.1.3.3.

The correct answer is C because the plural noun "students" matches the plural pronoun "they."

40. The correct answer is F (When the teacher collected their homework, there were five papers missing).

Item type: Cloze-based

Category: Conventions

©Copyright 2006 by Barron's Educational Series, Inc.

Benchmark: LA.B.1.3.3.

The correct answer is F because the homework belongs to them, so "their" should be used, and "there were" is the correct spelling.

41. The correct answer is B (Each of the students has a writing notebook for the entire year in Language Arts).

Item type: Cloze-based

Category: Conventions

Benchmark: LA.B.1.3.3.

The correct answer is B because the singular subject "each" matches the singular verb "has."

42. The correct answer is G (The trip to the Holocaust Museum in Washington DC lasted only a few hours; however, it left an impression on the students for a long time).

Item type: Cloze-based

Category: Conventions

Benchmark: LA.B.1.3.3.

The correct answer is G because a semicolon is necessary to separate two main clauses.

43. The correct answer is A (Having a hobby keeps Jose content, but his mom has to work longer hours so she has enough money for his supplies).

Item type: Stand-alone

Category: Conventions

Benchmark: LA.B.1.3.3.

The correct answer is A because a comma is necessary to separate two main clauses joined by the conjunction "but."

44. The correct answer is F (Dogs are so much cuter when they are puppies).

Item type: Stand-alone

Category: Conventions

Benchmark: LA.B.1.3.3.

The correct answer is F because the correct way to make "puppy" plural is to change the "y" to an "i" and add "es."

45. The correct answer is C (Being the only redhead and a boy, Jimmy stood out on stage when the choir sang).

Item type: Stand-alone

Category: Conventions

Benchmark: LA.B.1.3.3.

The correct answer is C because it is the only sentence that repeats the entire phrase "being the only."

FCAT PRACTICE TEST ONE ANSWER BOOKLET

Carefully remove this answer booklet and use it with Practice Test One P1: FCAT Reading and Writing+ Tests.

FCAT Reading Test

Directions: Fill in the bubble for the answer you choose for each multiple-choice question. For your response to READ/THINK/EXPLAIN questions, write your answer using complete sentences on the lines provided.

Beginning time: _____

1. Ⓐ Ⓑ Ⓒ Ⓓ   **2.** Ⓕ Ⓖ Ⓗ Ⓘ   **3.** Ⓐ Ⓑ Ⓒ Ⓓ
4. Ⓕ Ⓖ Ⓗ Ⓘ   **5.** Ⓐ Ⓑ Ⓒ Ⓓ   **6.** Ⓕ Ⓖ Ⓗ Ⓘ

7. READ/THINK/EXPLAIN Answer (extended response):

_____

_____

_____

_____

_____

_____

_____

8. Ⓐ Ⓑ Ⓒ Ⓓ   **9.** Ⓕ Ⓖ Ⓗ Ⓘ   **10.** Ⓐ Ⓑ Ⓒ Ⓓ
11. Ⓕ Ⓖ Ⓗ Ⓘ   **12.** Ⓐ Ⓑ Ⓒ Ⓓ   **13.** Ⓕ Ⓖ Ⓗ Ⓘ

©Copyright 2006 by Barron's Educational Series, Inc.

14. READ/THINK/EXPLAIN Answer (short response):

_____

_____

_____

_____

15. Ⓐ Ⓑ Ⓒ Ⓓ

16. READ/THINK/EXPLAIN Answer (short response):

_____

_____

_____

_____

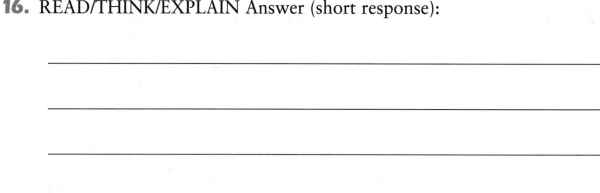

17. Ⓕ Ⓖ Ⓗ Ⓘ   **18.** Ⓐ Ⓑ Ⓒ Ⓓ   **19.** Ⓕ Ⓖ Ⓗ Ⓘ

20. Ⓐ Ⓑ Ⓒ Ⓓ   **21.** Ⓕ Ⓖ Ⓗ Ⓘ   **22.** Ⓐ Ⓑ Ⓒ Ⓓ

23. Ⓕ Ⓖ Ⓗ Ⓘ   **24.** Ⓐ Ⓑ Ⓒ Ⓓ   **25.** Ⓕ Ⓖ Ⓗ Ⓘ

26. READ/THINK/EXPLAIN Answer (short response):

_____

_____

_____

_____

27. READ/THINK/EXPLAIN Answer (extended response):

_____

_____

_____

_____

_____

_____

_____

28. Ⓐ Ⓑ Ⓒ Ⓓ   **29.** Ⓕ Ⓖ Ⓗ Ⓘ   **30.** Ⓐ Ⓑ Ⓒ Ⓓ

31. Ⓕ Ⓖ Ⓗ Ⓘ   **32.** Ⓐ Ⓑ Ⓒ Ⓓ

©Copyright 2006 by Barron's Educational Series, Inc.

33. READ/THINK/EXPLAIN Answer (short response):

_____

_____

_____

_____

_____

34. Ⓕ Ⓖ Ⓗ Ⓘ   **35.** Ⓐ Ⓑ Ⓒ Ⓓ   **36.** Ⓕ Ⓖ Ⓗ Ⓘ
37. Ⓐ Ⓑ Ⓒ Ⓓ   **38.** Ⓕ Ⓖ Ⓗ Ⓘ

39. READ/THINK/EXPLAIN Answer (short response):

_____

_____

_____

_____

40. Ⓐ Ⓑ Ⓒ Ⓓ   **41.** Ⓕ Ⓖ Ⓗ Ⓘ

42. READ/THINK/EXPLAIN Answer (extended response):

_____

_____

_____

_____

_____

_____

_____

_____

43. Ⓐ Ⓑ Ⓒ Ⓓ   **44.** Ⓕ Ⓖ Ⓗ Ⓘ   **45.** Ⓐ Ⓑ Ⓒ Ⓓ

Ending time: _____

©Copyright 2006 by Barron's Educational Series, Inc.

FCAT Writing+ Test (Essay)

Beginning time: _____

Planning Sheet

Essay Sheet

_____

_____

_____

_____

_____

_____

_____

_____

_____

_____

_____

_____

_____

_____

_____

_____

_____

_____

_____

_____

©Copyright 2006 by Barron's Educational Series, Inc.

_____

_____

_____

_____

_____

_____

_____

_____

_____

_____

_____

_____

_____

_____

_____

_____

_____

_____

_____

_____

_____

Ending time: _____

FCAT Writing+ Test (Multiple choice)
Directions: Fill in the bubble for the answer you choose for each multiple-choice question.

Beginning time: _____

1. Ⓐ Ⓑ Ⓒ Ⓓ

2. Ⓕ Ⓖ Ⓗ Ⓘ

3. Ⓐ Ⓑ Ⓒ Ⓓ

4. Ⓕ Ⓖ Ⓗ Ⓘ

5. Ⓐ Ⓑ Ⓒ Ⓓ

6. Ⓕ Ⓖ Ⓗ Ⓘ

7. Ⓐ Ⓑ Ⓒ Ⓓ

8. Ⓕ Ⓖ Ⓗ Ⓘ

9. Ⓐ Ⓑ Ⓒ Ⓓ

10. Ⓕ Ⓖ Ⓗ Ⓘ

11. Ⓐ Ⓑ Ⓒ Ⓓ

12. Ⓕ Ⓖ Ⓗ Ⓘ

13. Ⓐ Ⓑ Ⓒ Ⓓ

14. Ⓕ Ⓖ Ⓗ Ⓘ

15. Ⓐ Ⓑ Ⓒ Ⓓ

16. Ⓕ Ⓖ Ⓗ Ⓘ

17. Ⓐ Ⓑ Ⓒ Ⓓ

18. Ⓕ Ⓖ Ⓗ Ⓘ

19. Ⓐ Ⓑ Ⓒ Ⓓ

20. Ⓕ Ⓖ Ⓗ Ⓘ

21. Ⓐ Ⓑ Ⓒ Ⓓ

22. Ⓕ Ⓖ Ⓗ Ⓘ

23. Ⓐ Ⓑ Ⓒ Ⓓ

24. Ⓕ Ⓖ Ⓗ Ⓘ

25. Ⓐ Ⓑ Ⓒ Ⓓ

26. Ⓕ Ⓖ Ⓗ Ⓘ

27. Ⓐ Ⓑ Ⓒ Ⓓ

28. Ⓕ Ⓖ Ⓗ Ⓘ

29. Ⓐ Ⓑ Ⓒ Ⓓ

30. Ⓕ Ⓖ Ⓗ Ⓘ

31. Ⓐ Ⓑ Ⓒ

32. Ⓕ Ⓖ Ⓗ

33. Ⓐ Ⓑ Ⓒ

34. Ⓕ Ⓖ Ⓗ

©Copyright 2006 by Barron's Educational Series, Inc.

35. Ⓐ Ⓑ Ⓒ   41. Ⓐ Ⓑ Ⓒ

36. Ⓕ Ⓖ Ⓗ   42. Ⓕ Ⓖ Ⓗ

37. Ⓐ Ⓑ Ⓒ   43. Ⓐ Ⓑ Ⓒ

38. Ⓕ Ⓖ Ⓗ   44. Ⓕ Ⓖ Ⓗ

39. Ⓐ Ⓑ Ⓒ   45. Ⓐ Ⓑ Ⓒ

40. Ⓕ Ⓖ Ⓗ

Ending time: _____

FCAT READING TEST

Read the article "Nesting Turtles Suffer Passing Setbacks" before answering questions 1 through 7 in the P2: FCAT Reading Test answer book.

Nesting Turtles Suffer Passing Setbacks

L ast February, trawlers relocated 69 loggerhead sea turtles during another Navy dredging at the entrance of Port Canaveral in east Central Florida.

Monitors watching from the dredges try to spot turtles, manatees, and right whales to halt operations before the animals can be harmed. Dredges must stop pumping sand on the beach during prime turtle nesting season from May to November. The dredges have deflecting devices to push the turtles and other sea life aside.

But those can fail, as can attempts to match new sand with the old, another danger to the turtles.

Biologists say turtles are conditioned to the grain size and color of the sand, and to the shape of the beach. It's unknown what turtles do after they reject

GO ON →

©Copyright 2006 by Barron's Educational Series, Inc.

a new beach: whether they dump their eggs at sea or find more suitable sand elsewhere.

If the sand's too dark or too light, changes in its temperature can sway the sex ratio of turtle hatchlings. Darker, hotter sand yields more females; lighter, cooler sand means more males.

Turtles stop digging if the sand is too densely packed, often the case with new beaches because sand is piped in with so much water. This creates a firm bed that is further packed by bulldozers spreading the sand. The beaches must be raked to keep sand loose enough for turtles to dig.

But a hardened beach is only part of the problem, said Bob Ernest, a biologist with Ecological Associates Inc. of Jensen Beach. "There's something about a wide, flat beach that may not appeal to turtles," Ernest said. His firm found turtle nesting dropped along four miles of Hutchinson Island in Martin County after new beach was pumped there in the mid-1990s. Nesting fell the first two years after the project, but increased where erosion was the worst before the nourishment.

"The number of turtles that come up on the beach doesn't actually go down, but the number that nest does," Ernest said.

"It was just something about the shape of the beach. When these new beaches are built, they are kind of like in a box fashion."

If new beach is built to more than a 30- to 40-degree incline, turtles can't reach the dunes to nest. Many turn around after bumping into the sand cliffs that form at the tide line shortly after nourishment.

There's another threat during the first year after nourishment. Engineers build beaches high so they last longer. The higher elevation exposes turtles to beach lights they wouldn't otherwise see. As a result, hatchlings wander toward the lights and into roads, instead of the sea. "It's just something that was unexpected," said Sandy MacPherson, a marine turtle biologist with the National Marine Fisheries Service.

But a harder, higher, box-shaped beach is better than no beach, biologists admit.

"I'd have to say it's an overall positive," Witherington said. "It's just so messy and disruptive."

GO ON →

Base your answers to questions 1 through 7 on the article "Nesting Turtles Suffer Passing Setbacks."

1. From the article about sea turtles, the reader can conclude that biologists believe that
   A. sea turtles prefer higher beaches with hard sand.
   B. beach renourishment affects the nesting patterns of sea turtles.
   C. although altered beaches may not appeal to sea turtles, they still reproduce just as well as on unaltered beaches.
   D. sea turtle populations continue to decline because of erosion.

2. The main idea of this article is that
   F. dredging is safe for most ocean animals.
   G. dredging is dangerous for ocean animals.
   H. beach nourishment projects are helpful for sea turtles.
   I. beach nourishment projects are harmful to sea turtles.

3. Read the following sentence from the article:

   Four of the Kemp's Ridleys and both greens died during dredging at Fort Clinch Inlet, along Florida's northernmost barrier island.

   The word "dredging" means
   A. dragging sand from the bottom of the ocean.
   B. placing sand on the bottom of the ocean.
   C. removing sand from the beaches.
   D. placing sand on nourished beaches.

4. What is the author's purpose in writing this article about sea turtles?
   F. to give a brief history of problems with sea turtle nests
   G. to explain the different problems associated with nesting sea turtles
   H. to illustrate the destruction of Florida's beaches
   I. to define dredging according to the biologists

©Copyright 2006 by Barron's Educational Series, Inc.

GO ON →

5. READ/THINK/ EXPLAIN: Does the author believe dredging helps or hurts sea turtles? Use details and information from the article to support your answer.

6. A steep incline for turtles causes the following to happen:
   A. Turtles can't reach the dunes to nest.
   B. Turtles easily climb the sand cliffs.
   C. Turtles bump into the shoreline.
   D. All of the above

7. READ/THINK/ EXPLAIN: How has dredging affected the nesting of sea turtles over time? Use details and information from the article to support your answer.

GO ON →

Read the poem "O Captain, My Captain" before answering questions 8 through 16.

O Captain, My Captain

By Walt Whitman

O Captain! my Captain! our fear-
ful trip is done,
The ship has weather'd every rack,
the prize we sought is won,
The port is near, the bells I hear,
the people all exulting,
While follow eyes the steady keel,
the vessel grim and daring;
But O heart! heart! heart!
O the bleeding drops of red!
Where on the deck my Captain lies,
Fallen cold and dead.

O Captain! my Captain! rise up
and hear the bells;
Rise up—for you the flag is
flung—for you the bugle trills,
O Captain! my Captain! rise up
and hear the bells;
For you bouquets and ribbon'd
wreaths—for you the shores
crowding,
For you they call, the swaying
mass, their eager faces turning;
Here, Captain! dear father!
This arm beneath your head!

It is some dream that on the deck
You've fallen cold and dead.
My Captain does not answer, his
lips are pale and still,
My father does not feel my arm,
he has no pulse nor will;
The ship is anchor'd safe and
sound, its voyage closed and
done,
From fearful trip the victor ship
comes in with object won;
Exult, O shores! and ring, O bells!
But I, with mournful tread,
Walk the deck my Captain lies,
Fallen cold and dead.

©Copyright 2006 by Barron's Educational Series, Inc.

GO ON →

Base your answers to questions 8 through 16 on the poem "O Captain, My Captain."

8. Read the first few lines from the first stanza:

The ship has weather'd every rack, the prize we sought is won,

The port is near, the bells I hear, the people all exulting,

While follow eyes the steady keel, the vessel grim and daring;

The word "vessel" means
F. cup or glass
G. storage container
H. stage coach or covered wagon
I. ship or boat

9. Read these lines from stanza 6:

O Captain! my Captain! rise up and hear the bells;

Rise up—for you the flag is flung—for you the bugle trills,

O Captain! my Captain! our fearful trip is done,

Why does the author call for the captain to "rise up and hear the bells"?
A. The author doesn't want him to miss the sound of the bells.
B. The author wants him to be alive and to know that he has been victorious.
C. The author thinks the captain is ignoring the calling of the bells.
D. The author believes if the captain hears the bells, he will awake from his slumber.

GO ON →

10. What is the author's purpose in writing this poem?

F. _____to compare the death of the captain to that of a great leader

G. to demonstrate to the reader the effects of a captain's death on his crew

H. to inform the reader of the death of an important captain

I. to prove to the reader that a crew can go on without its captain.

11. The captain is compared to

A. a father.

B. his ship.

C. a prize.

D. none of the above

12. Which phrase best characterizes the captain?

F. militant leader

G. mournful servant

H. heroic, great leader

I. defeated captain

13. READ/THINK/ EXPLAIN: Explain the irony of the captain's death. Use details and examples from the poem to support your answer.

14. This purpose of this poem is to

A. inform the reader that a captain has died.

B. persuade the reader to feel sorry for the captain.

C. evoke emotion in the reader.

D. narrate a story to the reader.

15. Which word best captures the mood of this poem?

F. angry

G. hopeless

H. joyous

I. mournful

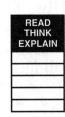

16. READ/THINK/ EXPLAIN: How does imagery contribute to the development of the poem? Use details and examples from the poem to support your answer.

©Copyright 2006 by Barron's Educational Series, Inc.

GO ON →

Read the short story excerpt from "The Treasure of Lemon Brown" before answering questions 17 through 24.

from The Treasure of Lemon Brown

By Walter Dean Myers

"You ain't one of them bad boys looking for my treasure, is you?" Lemon Brown cocked his head to one side and squinted one eye. "Because I told you I got me a razor."

"I'm not looking for your treasure," Greg answered, smiling. "*If* you have one."

"What you mean, *if* I have one," Lemon Brown said. "Every man got a treasure. You don't know that, you must be a fool!"

"Sure," Greg said as he sat on the sofa and put one leg over the back. "What do you have, gold coins?"

"Don't worry none about what I got," Lemon Brown said. "You know who I am?"

"You told me your name was orange or lemon or something like that."

"Lemon Brown," the old man said, pulling back his shoulders as he did so, "they used to call me Sweet Lemon Brown."

"Sweet Lemon?" Greg asked.

"Yessir. Sweet Lemon Brown. They used to say I sung the blues so sweet that if I sang at a funeral, the dead would commence to rocking with the beat. Used to travel all over Mississippi and as far as Monroe, Louisiana, and east on over to Macon, Georgia. You mean you ain't never heard of Sweet Lemon Brown?"

"Afraid not," Greg said.

GO ON →

"What . . . what happened to you?"

"Hard times, boy. Hard times always after a poor man. One day I got tired, sat down to rest a spell and felt a tap on my shoulder. Hard times caught up with me."

"Sorry about that."

"What you doing here? How come you didn't go on home when the rain come? Rain don't bother you young folks none."

"Just didn't." Greg looked away.

"I used to have a knotty-headed boy just like you." Lemon Brown had half walked, half shuffled back to the corner and sat down against the wall. "Had them big eyes like you got, I used to call them moon eyes. Look into them moon eyes and see anything you want."

"How come you gave up singing the blues?" Greg asked.

"Didn't give it up," Lemon Brown said. "You don't give up the blues; they give you up. After a while you do good for yourself, and it ain't nothing but foolishness singing about how hard you got it. Ain't that right?"

"I guess so."

"What's that noise?" Lemon Brown asked, suddenly sitting upright.

Greg listened, and he heard a noise outside. He looked at Lemon Brown and saw the old man pointing toward the window.

Greg went to the window and saw three men, neighborhood thugs, on the stoop. One was carrying a length of pipe. Greg looked back toward Lemon Brown, who moved quietly across the room to the window. The old man looked out, then beckoned frantically for Greg to follow him. For a moment Greg couldn't move. Then he found himself following Lemon Brown into the hallway and up darkened stairs. Greg followed as closely as he could. They reached the top of the stairs, and Greg felt Lemon Brown's hand first lying on his shoulder, then probing down his arm until he finally took Greg's hand into his own as they crouched in the darkness.

"They's bad men," Lemon Brown whispered. His breath was warm against Greg's skin.

"Hey! Rag man!" A voice called. "We know you in here. What you got up under them rags? You got any money?"

Silence.

"We don't want to have to come in and hurt you, old man, but we don't mind if we have to."

©Copyright 2006 by Barron's Educational Series, Inc.

GO ON →

Lemon Brown squeezed Greg's hand in his own hard, gnarled fist. There was a banging downstairs and a light as the men entered. They banged around noisily, calling for the rag man.

"We heard you talking about your treasure." The voice was slurred. "We just want to see it, that's all."

"You sure he's here?" One voice seemed to come from the room with the sofa.

"Yeah, he stays here every night."

"There's another room over there; I'm going to take a look. You got that flashlight?"

"Yeah, here, take the pipe too."

Greg opened his mouth to quiet the sound of his breath as he sucked it in uneasily. A beam of light hit the wall a few feet opposite him, then went out.

"Ain't nobody in that room," a voice said. "You think he gone or something?"

"I don't know," came the answer. "All I know is that I heard him talking about some kind of treasure. You know they found that shopping bag lady with that money in her bags."

"Yeah. You think he's upstairs?"

"HEY, OLD MAN, ARE YOU UP THERE?"

Silence.

"Watch my back, I'm going up."

There was a footstep on the stairs, and the beam from the flashlight danced crazily along the peeling wallpaper. Greg held his breath. There was another step and a loud crashing noise as the man banged the pipe against the wooden banister. Greg could feel his temples throb as the man slowly neared them. Greg thought about the pipe, wondering what he would do when the man reached them—what he *could* do.

GO ON →

Base your answers to questions 17 through 24 on the excerpt from "The Treasure of Lemon Brown."

17. What does Greg do when he sees that the owner of the voice is Lemon Brown?
A. He does nothing.
B. He yells out in fear.
C. He freezes.
D. He relaxes.

18. READ/THINK/EXPLAIN: What does Lemon Brown mean when he says "Every man got a treasure"? Use details and examples from the short story to support your answer.

19. Why did Lemon Brown stop singing the blues?
F. The blues gave up on him.
G. He was tired of singing the blues.
H. He wasn't good at singing the blues anymore.
I. He gave up singing the blues.

20. Why does Lemon Brown squeeze Greg's hand?
A. He was trying to hurt Greg.
B. Greg was trying to stop Lemon Brown.
C. Lemon Brown was comforting Greg.
D. Lemon Brown was a bit afraid.

21. What did Lemon Brown think the men were going to do with his treasure?
F. He thought they were going to give it away.
G. He thought they were going to sell it for a high price.
H. He thought they were going to hide it from him.
I. He thought they were going to steal it.

22. Read the following sentence from the short story:

Lemon Brown squeezed Greg's hand in his own hard, gnarled fist.

What does "gnarled" mean?
A. smaller than normal
B. rough and ragged
C. smooth
D. young and healthy

©Copyright 2006 by Barron's Educational Series, Inc.

GO ON →

23. What type of man is Lemon Brown?
   F. a lawyer
   G. a pirate
   H. a homeless man
   I. an apartment manager

24. READ/THINK/EXPLAIN: Explain the theme of the poem. Use details and examples from the short story to support your answer.

GO ON →

Read the folktale "Pecos Bill" and answer questions 25 through 32.

Pecos Bill

Retold by Mary Pope Osborne

When Pecos Bill was a little baby, he was as tough as a pine knot. He teethed on horseshoes instead of teething rings and played with grizzly bears instead of teddy bears. He could have grown up just fine in the untamed land of eastern Texas. But one day his pappy ran in from the fields, hollering, "Pack up, Ma! Neighbors movin' in fifty miles away! It's gettin' too crowded!"

Before sundown Bill's folks loaded their fifteen kids and all their belongings into their covered wagon and started west.

As they clattered across the desolate land of western Texas the crushing heat nearly drove them all crazy. Baby Bill got so hot and cross that he began to wallop his big brothers. Pretty soon all fifteen kids were going at one another tooth and nail. Before they turned each other into catfish bait, Bill fell out of the wagon and landed kerplop on the sun-scorched desert.

The others were so busy fighting that they didn't even notice the baby was missing until it was too late to do anything about it.

Well, tough little Bill just sat there in the dirt, watching his family rattle off in a cloud of dust, until an old coyote walked over and sniffed him.

"Goo-goo!" Bill said.

Now it's an amazing coincidence, but "Goo-goo" happens to mean something similar to "Glad to meet you" in coyote language. Naturally the old coyote figured he'd come across one of his own kind. He gave Bill a

©Copyright 2006 by Barron's Educational Series, Inc.

GO ON →

big lick and picked him up by the scruff of the neck and carried him home to his den. Bill soon discovered the coyote's kinfolk were about the wildest, roughest bunch you could imagine. Before he knew it, he was roaming the prairies with the pack. He howled at the moon, sniffed the brush, and chased lizards across the sand. He was having such a good time, scuttling about naked and dirty on all fours, that he completely forgot what it was like to be human.

—*Copyright Colin Poole, Language of Literature, McDougal Littell.*

Base your answers to questions 25 through 32 on the folktale "Pecos Bill."

25. This story takes place when Pecos Bill
   A. was an infant.
   B. was a teenager.
   C. was an adult.
   D. was about to die.

26. Which sentence below contains an example of onomatopoeia?
   F. Pack up, Ma! Neighbors movin' in fifty miles away!
   G. Naturally the old coyote figured he'd come across one of his own kind. He gave Bill a big lick and picked him up by the scruff of the neck and carried him home to his den.
   H. Before they turned each other into catfish bait, Bill fell out of the wagon and landed kerplop on the sun-scorched desert.
   I. He was having such a good time, scuttling about naked and dirty on all fours, that he completely forgot what it was like to be human.

GO ON ➔

27. In the last paragraph, "Googoo" means
A. "My name is . . ."
B. "Goodbye."
C. "Nice to meet you."
D. None of the above

28. Pecos Bill's family lost him when they were
F. traveling to the east.
G. went on vacation.
H. moving out west.
I. had another baby.

29. Pecos Bill was raised by
A. a pack of coyotes.
B. his ma and pa.
C. his 14 brothers and sisters.
D. no one.

30. Pecos Bill did all of the following EXCEPT
F. howl.
G. sniff.
H. chase lizards.
I. act like a baby.

31. READ/THINK/EXPLAIN: How did Pecos Bill lose his family? Use details and examples from the tale to support your answer.

32. READ/THINK/EXPLAIN: What type of literary devices are used in this tall tale? Use details and examples from the tale to support your answer.

©Copyright 2006 by Barron's Educational Series, Inc.

GO ON →

Read the article "A Brief Summary of Seminole History" before answering questions 33 through 40.

A Brief Summary of Seminole History

For thousands of years before the coming of Europeans to southeastern North America, perhaps as many as 400,000 of the ancestors of the Seminoles built towns and villages and complex civilizations across the vast area. After 1510, when the Spaniards began to explore and settle in their territory, disease killed many of these people, but they were never "destroyed" or "conquered" as so many of the white men's history books proclaim. The survivors amalgamated across the peninsula of Florida and continued their lives.

When the first English speakers entered the area of the Southeast that is now Florida, in 1763, they found many of these survivors—from tribes such as the Euchee, Yamasee, Timugua, Tequesta, Abalachi, Coça, and hundreds of others, living as "free people" across the head of the Florida peninsula, on the Alachua savannah (the area now known as Alachua County). In Maskókî, the core language, *istî siminolî* meant that they were "free people" because they had never been dominated by the Spaniards or the English interlopers. In the Hitchíti dialect of Maskókî, today known as Mikisúkî, the same phrase was *yat'siminoli*. English speakers

GO ON →

ignored their separate tribal affiliations and just called them all Seminolies, or Seminoles.

With the end of the American Revolutionary War and the creation of the United States in 1784, white settlers moved steadily southward into the Spanish and former English colonies. It became more and more obvious that a clash between white immigrants and the Native inhabitants of the land would take place sooner or later. The new US began a concerted policy of taking or buying land from the Native tribes in the Northeast and the Atlantic seaboard states. By 1813, some of the Maskókî tribes in Alabama rose up against the white settlers and against those other tribes that supported white setlement. This conflict, known as the Creek War of 1813–14, was disastrous to the cultural relatives of the Seminoles. General, later president, Andrew Jackson, brought US troops to crush the uprising and forced a treaty on the Creeks that took over 2,000,000 acres of land away from his foes and his allies alike. Several thousand Maskókî people, warriors and their wives and children, lost their homes and migrated southward into Spanish Florida where they and

the Seminoles increased their resistance to continued white settlement.

Over the next few years, Jackson illegally entered Spanish Florida to burn Native villages and kill resistance leaders. After the first series of encounters, known as the First Seminole War (1814–18), many Native families moved further into the peninsula. By 1820, the year before Spanish Florida became a US Territory, there were at least 5,000 Seminoles, "Creeks," and Mikisúkî people living in Florida. But a series of treaties made in the 1820s and early 1830s failed to protect the rights of Florida's Native people and, by late 1835, war broke out again.

This one, the Second Seminole War (1835–42), would be the longest, most costly, and the last of the US's Wars of Indian Removal fought east of the Mississippi River. It would be the first "guerilla"-style war fought by US troops. Not until the US entered a tiny country in Southeast Asia called Vietnam, more than a century later, would US soldiers fight again under such profoundly difficult conditions. The Natives were aided in their resistance by runaway slaves, who received protection

©Copyright 2006 by Barron's Educational Series, Inc.

GO ON →

from their Seminole allies (and, in some cases, owners) in return for a portion of the agricultural staples that they grew. These so-called "Black Seminoles" were fierce fighters who were also determined to preserve their freedom.

Their descendants remained isolated in the Everglades until the late 1800s, when white traders, Christian missionaries, and US government agents began to enter their territory once again. From the 1920s onward, as the development Boom exploded in South Florida, the Seminoles lost more and more of their hunting lands to tourists and settlers and were slowly forced into a wage economy. They became agricultural work-ers in the vegetable fields of South Florida, and tourist attractions, in their unique and colorful patchwork clothing, producing souvenirs and "wrestling" alligators for the tourists.

Today, there are about 500 members of this Tribe. The Seminole Tribe of Florida has almost 3,000 members, living on five reservations across the peninsula at Hollywood (formerly Dania), Big Cypress, Brighton, Immokalee, and Tampa. The Tribe obtains significant annual gross revenues from such diverse economic sources as agriculture, citrus, aircraft production, gaming, tobacco sales, land leases, cattle, and aquaculture.

Base your answers to questions 33 through 40 on the article "A Brief Summary of Seminole History."

33. When did the Creek War take place?
A. late 1600s
B. mid-1700s
C. early 1800s
D. late 1800s

34. Why did many Native families move further into the peninsula?
F. to escape the effects of the First Seminole War
G. to find better places to build their communities
H. to live out the conditions of a treaty
I. to find a way to make a living

GO ON →

35. Who aided the Natives in their resistance in the early 1800s?
A. Christian missionaries
B. runaway slaves
C. white traders
D. the original Seminole indian tribe

36. READ/THINK/EXPLAIN: Where does the Seminoles' name come from? Use details and examples from the story in your answer.

37. Which war lasted the longest and cost the most money for the Seminole Indians?
F. the French and Indian War
G. the Creek War
H. the First Seminole War
I. the Second Seminole War

38. According to the article, all of the following are places the Florida Seminoles live today EXCEPT
A. Hollywood.
B. Big Cypress.
C. Tampa.
D. Tallahassee.

39. Who entered the Seminoles' territory in the late 1800s?
F. Christian missionaries
G. U.S. government agents
H. white traders
I. all of the above

40. Who was the first group to settle Florida?
A. Christian missionaries
B. Seminole Indians
C. Spaniards
D. white traders

©Copyright 2006 by Barron's Educational Series, Inc.

GO ON →

Read the article "A New Mode of Transportation: Space Elevators" and answer questions 41 through 45.

A New Mode of Transportation: Space Elevators

NASA scientists are seriously considering space elevators as a mass-transit system for the next century.

"Yes, ladies and gentlemen, welcome aboard NASA's *Millennium-Two Space Elevator*. Your first stop will be the Lunar-level platform before we continue on to the New Frontier Space Colony development. The entire ride will take about 5 hours, so sit back and enjoy the trip. As we rise, be sure to watch outside the window as the curvature of the Earth becomes visible and the sky changes from deep blue to black, truly one of the most breathtaking views you will ever see!"

It is a real possibility—a "space elevator"—that researchers are considering today as a far-out space transportation system for the next century. Four to six "elevator tracks" would extend up the sides of the tower and cable structure going to platforms at different levels. These tracks would allow electromagnetic vehicles to travel at speeds reaching thousands of kilometers-per-hour.

Conceptual designs place the

GO ON →

tower construction at an equatorial site. The extreme height of the lower tower section makes it vulnerable to high winds. An equatorial location is ideal for a tower of such enormous height because the area is practically devoid of hurricanes and tornadoes and it aligns properly with geostationary orbits (which are directly overhead).

According to Smitherman, construction is not feasible today but it could be toward the end of the 21st century. "First we'll develop the technology," said Smitherman. "In 50 years or so, we'll be there. Then, if the need is there, we'll be able to do this. That's the gist of the report."

The builders use advanced materials such as the carbon nanofibers now in laboratory study.

Pearson, who participated in the 1999 workshop, envisions the space elevator as a cost-cutting device for NASA. "One of the fundamental problems we face right now is that it's so unbelievably expensive to get things into orbit," said Pearson. "The space elevator may be the answer."

The workshop's findings determined the energy required to move a payload by space elevator from the ground to geostationary orbit could remain relatively low. Using today's energy costs, researchers figured a 12,000-kg Space Shuttle payload would cost no more than $17,700 for an elevator trip to GEO. A passenger with baggage at 150 kg might cost only $222! "Compare that to today's cost of around $10,000 per pound ($22,000 per kg)," said Smitherman. "Potentially, we're talking about just a few dollars per kg with the elevator."

©Copyright 2006 by Barron's Educational Series, Inc.

GO ON →

Base your answers to questions 41 through 45 on the article "A New Mode of Transportation: Space Elevators."

41. How fast would the space elevators need to travel in order to get into space?
F. thousands of miles per hour
G. thousands of meters per hour
H. thousands of kilometers per hour
I. thousands of nanometers per hour

42. Another name for a space elevator is
A. elevator track.
B. geostationary orbit.
C. electromagnetic vehicle.
D. platform.

43. The first time a workshop was held discussing the idea of space elevators was in
F. the early 1900s.
G. the 1960s.
H. late 1990.
I. early 2000.

44. The main purpose for creating space elevators is to
A. cut costs for NASA.
B. provide a more high-class travel experience.
C. make space accessible to every human.
D. create a community on the moon.

45. READ/THINK/ EXPLAIN: Is it really possible that a space elevator will be built? Use details and examples from the article to support your answer.

This is the end of the FCAT Reading Test. Record the time in your answer booklet so that you can determine how long it took you to take this test. If it took you longer than the allowed 160 minutes, you must work on reading the passages and answering the questions more quickly.

FCAT Writing+ Test (Essay)

Writing Situation: *Your parents want your opinion on whether or not you should have your own cell phone.*

Directions for Writing: *Before you begin to write, decide whether or not you should have your own cell phone. Then write to convince your parents of your opinion. Support your ideas with examples and details.*

This is the end of the Writing+ Test (Essay).

Record the time in your answer booklet so that you can determine how long it took you to take this test. If it took you longer than the allowed 45 minutes, you should work on planning, writing, and proofreading/editing your essay more quickly.

©Copyright 2006 by Barron's Educational Series, Inc.

FCAT WRITING+ TEST (MULTIPLE CHOICE)

Mark made the writing plan below to organize ideas for a paper he is writing. Read the writing plan and answer questions 1 through 3.

The Civil War

Major battles
  Second Bull Run
  Fredericksburg
  Gettysburg

Important people
  Stonewall Jackson
  Abraham Lincoln
  Robert E. Lee

Results of war
Casualties

1. Under which subtopic should details about generals and commanders be placed?
    A. Important battles
    B. Important people
    C. Results of war
    D. None of the above

2. Based on the writing plan, what kind of paper is Mark planning to write?
    F. a paper that compares the Civil War with the French and Indian War
    G. a paper that explains and summarizes the major points of the Civil War
    H. a paper that persuades the reader to agree with the Union side
    I. a paper that persuades the reader to agree with the Confederate side

3. Which detail below supports the subtopic "Results of war"?
    A. thousands of deaths
    B. a divided country
    C. divided families
    D. all of the above

GO ON →

Rosa made the outline below to organize ideas for a paper she is writing. Some of the details under the subtopics have not been listed yet. Read the writing plan and answer questions 4 through 6.

Music Affects Learning

I. Good effects

II. Bad effects
   A.
   B.

III. Classical music helps learning
   A.
   B.

IV. Heavy metal music hinders learning
   A.
   B.

4. According to Rosa, which details should be listed under the third subtopic?
   F. Beethoven, Bach, Chopin
   G. Rap, heavy metal, rock n' roll
   H. boring, dull, sleepy
   I. fast, rapid, crazy

5. The subtopics of this formal outline indicate that the topic would NOT be too
   A. short for a research paper.
   B. broad for an essay.
   C. vague for a personal letter.
   D. detailed for an editorial.

6. Under which subtopic should details about the benefits of listening to music be placed?
   F. Good effects
   G. Bad effects
   H. Classical music helps learning
   I. Heavy metal music hinders learning

GO ON →

The essay below is a first draft that Darnel wrote for his teacher. The essay contains errors. Read the essay and answer questions 7 through 12.

Second Hand Smoke Really Is Dangerous

[1] Second hand smoke is dangerous for several reasons. [2] When kids have allergies or asthma, it's important not to smoke around them. [3] Also, it can make any non-smoker uncomfortable. [4] Finally, you could even get a serious disease from second hand smoke.

[5] First of all, if you have asthma, it will irritate it even more. [6] All the coughing can trigger an attack, which is very scary. [7] Because I have severe asthma, it is almost instantly affected by second hand smoke. [8] Not being able to breathe makes me feel like I'm dying. [9] If it weren't for second hand smoke, I wouldn't have to carry my inhaler around with me at all times. [10] Even if I use the inhaler to help my breathing, I still have to contact my doctor right away.

[11] Then theirs the coughing from the burning sensation in your throat as the second hand smoke enters the body. [12] No

one likes that itchy, scratchy feeling. [13] Not even cough drops will help.

[14] Finally, there are some studies out today that say you can even get cancer from second hand smoke! [15] I don't think that's fair, though. [16] I mean, if I decide not to smoke, but other people do and I get sick, it's just not fair.

[17] I think it's about time we asked people not to smoke around non-smokers. [18] Hopefully many business and restaurants will ban smoking indoors. [19] I know airports already have designated areas.

GO ON →

7. Which sentence contains a spelling error?
   A. sentence 2
   B. sentence 6
   C. sentence 11
   D. sentence 14

8. Which sentence should be deleted from paragraph 2 to maintain the focus?
   F. sentence 5
   G. sentence 7
   H. sentence 8
   I. sentence 10

9. Which sentence should be deleted because it presents a detail that is unrelated to the main points of the essay?
   A. sentence 3
   B. sentence 11
   C. sentence 17
   D. sentence 19

10. Darnel wants to add the sentence below to his essay:

We should educate smokers about the dangers of second hand smoke.

Where should this sentence be added to keep the details in the correct order?
   F. at the end of paragraph 1
   G. at the beginning of paragraph 2
   H. at the end of paragraph 3
   I. at the end of paragraph 4

11. Which sentence below should Darnel add to conclude his essay with a summary?
   A. Many other places should have designated areas, too.
   B. Let's do what we can to prevent the dangers of second hand smoke.
   C. Now it's time for places like malls to ban smoking, too.
   D. There are serious health risks for the smokers, too.

12. Why does Darnel organize his essay the way he does?
   F. He wants to convince the reader to make a stand against secondhand smoke.
   G. He wants to explain three major effects of smoking.
   H. He wants to list reasons why people should not smoke.
   I. He wants to explain why people get cancer.

©Copyright 2006 by Barron's Educational Series, Inc.

GO ON →

The paragraphs below are just the first few for an essay Mike will write for his teacher. The essay is incomplete and contains errors. Read the essay and answer questions 13 through 18.

The Misadventures of Jolly, the Gerbil

[1] I named my gerbil Jolly because she looks like a plump little elf! [2] A couple of months after I got Jolly, she gave birth to four little gerbils. [3] I guess that's why she was so plump when I first got her.

[4] Some of the things Jolly loves to do include run in her cage and sit on her babies. [5] She can run and sit for hours at a time. [6] She seems so content; she almost looks like she's smiling at me when she twitches her nose back and forth. [7] But every now and then, Jolly hides in the corner and seems sad.

[8] One day she got out of her cage and caused alot of problems in the house. [9] First, she

got stuck in the couch cushions but my cat helped her get free! [10] Jolly was so scared, I've never seen her run so fast in my life. [11] But she did make it back to my room and I shut the door behind her just before my cat caught her.

GO ON →

13. Which sentence below matches the tone of Mike's essay?
- **A.** Jolly happens to be my most adored creature to date.
- **B.** Jolly is my favorite pet.
- **C.** I have never enjoyed a gerbil as much as I adore Jolly.
- **D.** Jolly's "da bomb."

14. Read the following sentence from Mike's essay:

One day she got out of her cage and caused alot of problems in the house.

Which revision below improves this sentence by correcting the spelling error?
- **F.** One day she got out of her cage and caused allot of problems in the house.
- **G.** One day she got out of her cage and cawsed alot of problems in the house.
- **H.** One day she got out of her cage and caused a lot of problems in the house.
- **I.** One day she got out of her cage and cawsed a lot of problems in the house.

15. Which sentence below should be deleted from paragraph 2?
- **A.** sentence 7
- **B.** sentence 6
- **C.** sentence 5
- **D.** sentence 4

16. Mike wants to add another paragraph to his essay. Choose a topic sentence below that could follow the third paragraph logically.
- **F.** I have been thinking about buying another gerbil since I gave away Jolly's babies to my friends and neighbors.
- **G.** Before her babies grow up, Jolly seems to be spending a lot of time sitting on them.
- **H.** When I first bought Jolly, she had a very small cage.
- **I.** Another time when Jolly got out of her cage, she scared my mother in the kitchen.

17. Which transitional sentence should be added at the beginning of the second paragraph to show the connection between the ideas in the essay?
- **A.** I also named her Jolly because of the way she spends her time.
- **B.** Another time when Jolly caused trouble happened just yesterday.
- **C.** In addition to her cute name, Jolly has very cute babies.
- **D.** When I picked Jolly up from the pet store, I knew I had a best friend.

©Copyright 2006 by Barron's Educational Series, Inc.

GO ON →

18. Read the sentence below from Mike's essay:

Jolly was so scared, I've never seen her run so fast in my life.

Which revision below improves this sentence by correcting the punctuation?

F. Jolly was so scared. . . . I've never seen her run so fast in my life.

G. Jolly was so scared; I've never seen her run so fast in my life.

H. Jolly was so scared: I've never seen her run so fast in my life.

I. Jolly was so scared—I've never seen her run so fast in my life.

GO ON →

The essay below is a first draft that Tyra wrote for her teacher. The essay contains errors. Read the essay and answer questions 19 through 24.

How to Start a Babysitting Business

[1] I really want to buy a mountain bike, but they're just so expensive. [2] So, I decided to earn the money on my own. [3] Since America is the land of opportunity, I set out to start my own business.

[4] First, I had to come up with a money making idea. [5] Not that many people would stop and buy lemonade or cookies on my street, so I ruled out a food and beverage business. [6] I'm not strong enough to push a lawn mower on my own, yet, so I decided against a lawn service company. [7] Then it hit me! [8] I'm great with kids, so I began working on a babysitting service. [9] Another idea I had was to sell bracelets.

[10] I needed to come up with a name that was catchy, so I settled on Tyras' tots. [11] Then I figured a catchy slogan would help my business be remembered. [12] I thought "She cares

for your kids" sounded like something that a parent would be looking for in a babysitter.

[13] After creating a name and slogan, it was then time to get the word out! [14] I created a poster in the computer lab after school. [15] Then I took it to a local office store to get copies made. [16] At only 3 cents a copy, I had made my first investment in my company.

©Copyright 2006 by Barron's Educational Series, Inc.

GO ON →

[17] Once I started hanging the posters in local grocery stores, and other places around town, the phone was ringing off the hook. [18] I had so many clients that I had to hire two extra workers to help me keep up with my business.

[19] Today I have four babysitters working for me in my business. [20] Each of us have regular clients.

19. Which sentence should be deleted because it presents a detail that is unimportant to the essay?
   A. the last sentence of paragraph 3
   B. the first sentence of paragraph 1
   C. the last sentence of paragraph 2
   D. the first sentence of paragraph 4

20. Read the following sentence from Tyra's essay:

   I needed to come up with a name that was catchy, so I settled on Tyras' tots.

   Which revision below improves the sentence by correcting the errors?
   F. I needed to come up with a name that was catchy, so I settled on "Tyra's Tots."
   G. I needed to come up with a name that was catchy, so I settled on "Tyras' tots."
   H. I needed to come up with a name that was catchy, so I settled on Tyras' Tots.
   I. I needed to come up with a name that was catchy, so I settled on Tyra's Tots.

GO ON →

21. Read the following sentence from Tyra's essay:

Each of us have regular clients.

Which revision below improves the sentence by correcting the grammatical error?
A. Each of us, we, has regular clients.
B. Each of us has regular clients.
C. Each of us, we, have regular clients.
D. Each of us had regular clients.

22. Which transition should be added at the beginning of paragraph 3 to show the connection between the ideas in the essay?
F. First of all,
G. Then
H. The next step was that
I. Before I could be open for business,

23. Read the following sentence from Tyra's essay:

After creating a name and slogan, it was then time to get the word out!

Which revision below improves this sentence by correcting the sentence structure?
A. After creating a name and slogan, the posters were ready to be made!
B. Because I created a name and slogan, it was then time to get the word out!
C. It was then time to get the word out because of creating a name and slogan.
D. After creating a name and slogan, I needed to get the word out!

24. Which sentence below should be added to conclude the essay?
F. After this success, I went on to start another business.
G. The best part is that I'm very close to having enough money to buy that mountain bike.
H. I'll never know if I can achieve my dreams or not.
I. The mountain bike went up in cost, and I wasn't able to buy it.

©Copyright 2006 by Barron's Educational Series, Inc.

GO ON →

The announcement below is a first draft that Jamal wrote for his school's Drama Club. The announcement contains errors. Read the announcement and answer questions 25 through 30.

Attention Future Thesbians:

[1] Tryouts for the eighth grade drama presentation, *The Diary of Anne Frank*, will be held next week after school in the Theatre from Monday until Wednesday. [2] The official cast will be announced Friday morning by this year's student director, James Thomas. [3] To audition, students must prepare a 3–5 minute monologue. [4] Students in the sixth and seventh grades are not allowed to try out. [5] Based on inflection, talent, and presentation, the play's director will decide which students make the cast.

[6] All students interested must pick up an application packet from one of the drama teachers by the afternoon and bring it completed to the audition, or they will not be eligible to audition. [7] Without a completed packet, students will not be permitted to try out. [8]

When picking up an application packet, students will be randomly assigned an audition time. [9] It is important that students do not bring anything to the audition—just bring yourself! [10] Each student will be asked his preference for a role in the production. [11] Fifteen cast members will be chosen to perform in the play.

[12] The drama club is also looking for stage hands and production assistants. [13] A total

GO ON →

of 30 students are needed in order to put on this production. [14] Only 5 people will have small parts, the rest are pretty important. [15] Good luck to everyone!

25. Read the following sentence from Jamal's announcement:

Tryouts for the eighth grade drama presentation, *The Diary of Anne Frank*, will be held next week after school in the Theatre from Monday until Wednesday.

Which revision below improves the sentence by correcting the spelling or capitalization error(s)?

A. Tryouts for the eigth grade drama presentation, *The Diary of Anne Frank*, will be held next week after school in the Theatre from Monday until Wednesday.

B. Tryouts for the eigth grade drama presentation, *The Diary of Anne Frank*, will be held next week after school in the theatre from Monday until Wednesday.

C. Tryouts for the eighth grade drama presentation, *The Diary of Anne Frank*, will be held next week after school in the Theatre from Monday until Wednesday.

D. Tryouts for the eighth grade drama presentation, *The Diary of Anne Frank*, will be held next week after school in the theatre from Monday until Wednesday.

26. Which sentence states information already presented and should be deleted from the announcement?

F. sentence 9
G. sentence 8
H. sentence 7
I. sentence 6

©Copyright 2006 by Barron's Educational Series, Inc.

GO ON →

27. Which transition should be added at the beginning of sentence 12 to show the connection between ideas in the announcement?

  A. In addition to cast members,
  B. After choosing cast members,
  C. Then,
  D. Without cast members,

28. Which revision below contains a necessary detail for sentence 6?

  F. All students interested must pick up an application packet from one of the drama teachers by Friday afternoon and bring it completed to the audition, or they will not be eligible to audition.
  G. All students interested must pick up an application packet from one of the drama teachers by the midafternoon and bring it to the audition, or they will not be eligible to audition.
  H. All students interested must pick up an application packet from one of the drama teachers by the afternoon and bring it to the audition, or they will not be eligible to audition.
  I. All students interested must pick up an application packet from one of the drama teachers by the afternoon and bring it completed to the audition, or they will not be eligible to audition.

29. Read the following sentence from the announcement:

It is important that students do not bring anything to the audition—just bring yourself!

Which word(s) should replace "anything" in sentence 9 to make the wording more specific?

  A. special clothing
  B. papers
  C. stuff
  D. props

30. Which sentence contains an unimportant detail that should be deleted from the announcement?

  F. sentence 12
  G. sentence 13
  H. sentence 14
  I. sentence 15

GO ON ➔

Read the article "Protect Florida's Gentle Giants" and answer questions 31 through 36.

Protect Florida's Gentle Giants

Also known as gentle giants, Florida manatees are curious creatures who live in rivers, estuaries, and inshore areas of Florida where the waters are warm. In fact, they cannot survive in colder waters. That is why it is important for us to be aware of the dangers we can leave behind for the manatee. If we educate ourselves, we will be able to protect them from future threats to their survival.

Another nickname for the manatee is "sea cow." Just like a "regular" cow, the main diet of a manatee is (31)_____, making it a herbivore. Many times manatee are sighted feeding in a sea grass bed. Vital to (32) _____ survival, the sea grass beds are being destroyed by pollution in the state.

We must educate ourselves in how to protect these (33) _____. In order to do that, we must be aware of the major threats to the manatee. The first threat is the large number of people moving into Florida on a daily basis. When people (34) _____ into an area, two things happen: there is more pollution and more boat traffic.

Another threat to the manatee is injury from boats. Because

©Copyright 2006 by Barron's Educational Series, Inc.

GO ON →

they can only swim 3–5 miles per hour, they are not fast enough to move out of the way of boaters. Yet another threat is injury from litter. Many common items that we bring to the water can be very hazardous to the manatee, including fishing equipment and refreshments. (35)_____ the plastic ring surrounding six packs can get tangled on a manatee.

So the next time you head to the water, be aware of these amazing creatures. Look for (36) _____, but do not leave anything that could harm the gentle giants.

31. Which answer should go in blank 31?
   A. meat
   B. plants
   C. herbs

32. Which answer should go in blank 32?
   F. their
   G. they're
   H. there

33. Which answer should go in blank 33?
   A. sea cows
   B. Sea cows
   C. Sea Cows

34. Which answer should go in blank 34?
   F. have been moving
   G. are moving
   H. move

35. Which answer should go in blank 35?
   A. For example,
   B. for example,
   C. For example

36. Which answer should go in blank 36?
   F. him
   G. them
   H. it

GO ON →

Read the questions below; answer questions 37 and 45 on your Sample Answer Sheet.

37. In which sentence below is all the capitalization correct?
A. Florida's rivers and protected forests provide a natural habitat for many animals.
B. Florida's rivers and Protected Forests provide a natural habitat for many animals.
C. Florida's rivers and protected forests provide a natural Habitat for many animals.

38. In which sentence below is the sentence structure effective?
F. Proud of her achievement, Jennie's report card was shown to everyone.
G. Proud of her own achievement, everyone saw Jennie's report card.
H. Proud of her achievement, Jennie showed everyone her excellent report card.

39. In which sentence below are all the grammar and usage correct?
A. The teacher asked everyone to turn in their homework.
B. The teacher asked everyone to turn in his or her homework.
C. The teacher asked everyone to turn in her homework.

40. In which sentence below are all the grammar and usage correct?
F. With a new head coach, the football team is expected to play well this year.
G. With a new head coach, the football team is expected to play good this year.
H. With a new head coach, the football team are expected to play well this year.

41. In which sentence below is all the capitalization correct?
A. NASA plans to expand its research on several planets including mars and saturn.
B. Nasa plans to expand its research on several Planets including Mars and Saturn.
C. NASA plans to expand its research on several planets including Mars and Saturn.

GO ON →

42. In which sentence below is all the punctuation correct?
- **F.** The following items must be retrieved from the store, toothpaste, hand soap, shampoo and conditioner.
- **G.** The following items must be retrieved from the store: toothpaste, hand soap, shampoo, and conditioner.
- **H.** The following items must be retrieved from the store; toothpaste, hand soap, shampoo, and conditioner.

43. In which sentence below is all the spelling correct?
- **A.** When writing an essay, it is important to write a clear topic sentence for each paragraph, witch indicates the main idea to the reader.
- **B.** When writing an essay, it is important to write a clear topic sentence for each paragraph, which indicates the main idea to the reader.
- **C.** When writing an essay, it is important to write a clear topic sentence for each paragraph, wich indicates the main idea to the reader.

44. In which sentence below is all the sentence structure correct?
- **F.** The newspaper reporter was asked to write his news story thoroughly, accurately, and quickly.
- **G.** The newspaper reporter was asked to write his news story thoroughly, accurately, and on time.
- **H.** The newspaper reporter was asked to write his news story quickly, accurately, and with lots of details.

45. In which sentence below are all the grammar and usage correct?
- **A.** Last year, my family have moved to Central Florida.
- **B.** Last year, my family will move to Central Florida.
- **C.** Last year, my family moved to Central Florida.

This is the end of the Writing+ Test (Multiple Choice). Record the time in your answer booklet so that you can determine how long it took you to take this test. If it took you longer than the allowed 90 minutes, you should work on reading the passages and answering the questions quicker.

FCAT READING TEST ANSWERS AND EXPLANATIONS

Note to students:
As you read through the correct answers, pay close attention to the explanations of the answers. The Florida Sunshine State Standards listed as benchmarks for each question tell you what type of skill is being tested in the question. (A complete list of the benchmarks can be found in the Appendix.)

Note to parents and teachers:
Pay close attention to the benchmarks listed. They indicate the type of skill being tested in each particular question according to the Florida Sunshine State Standards. Use these skills to provide similar practice before the test. (A complete list of the benchmarks can be found in the Appendix.)

1. The correct answer is B (beach nourishment affects the nesting patterns of sea turtles).

Type of passage: Informational text

Benchmark: LA.A.2.3.1

The correct answer is B. Throughout the article, biologists mention how turtles reject nourished beaches and how nesting drops after nourishment. None of the other choices mention that turtles' nesting patterns are affected.

2. The correct answer is I (beach nourishment projects are harmful to sea turtles).

Type of passage: Informational text

Benchmark: LA.A.2.3.1

The correct answer is I. There are several points mentioned about how beach nourishment projects are harmful to the nesting patterns of sea turtles, supporting the main idea about how harmful nourishment projects are to sea turtles overall.

©Copyright 2006 by Barron's Educational Series, Inc.

3. The correct answer is A (dragging sand from the bottom of the ocean).

Type of passage: Informational text

Benchmark: LA.A.1.3.2.

The correct answer is A. Dredging is the act of removing sand from the bottom of the ocean and moving it to the beach, making the beach larger. This answer choice is the only one that matches the definition.

4. The correct answer is G (to explain the different problems associated with nesting sea turtles).

Type of passage: Informational text

Benchmark: LA.A.2.2.2

The correct answer is G. The author lists several problems for nesting sea turtles: Higher beaches with a steeper incline make it difficult for nesting turtles; harder sand deters nesting sea turtles. This is the only choice that mentions the problems for nesting sea turtles.

5. Use the short-response scoring rubric in Chapter 5 to score this response (2-point scoring rubric).

Type of passage: Informational text

Benchmark: LA.A.2.3.2

A top-score response would include at least one reason why dredging harms sea turtles.

For example:

The author believes that the dredging hurts the sea turtles because it makes the sand too hard for them to dig a nest. When they put the new sand on the beach, they pile it too high for the turtles to climb and make a nest.

6. The correct answer is A (Turtles can't reach the dunes to nest).

Type of passage: Informational text

Benchmark: LA.E.2.2.1

The correct answer is A. The article states, "If new beach is built to more than a 30- to 40-degree incline, turtles can't reach the dunes to nest." This is the only answer choice that mentions that the incline keeps the turtles from nesting.

7. Use the extended-response scoring rubric in Chapter 5 to score this response (4-point scoring rubric).

Type of passage: Informational text

Benchmark: LA.A.1.3.4.

A top-score response would list the ways dredging has affected the nesting of sea turtles over time, including the great decline in nesting turtle populations after a nourishment project. For example:

Dredging has greatly affected the nesting of sea turtles over time. First of all, the altered beaches confuse the turtles. They find it difficult to travel up the steeper inclines created by the dredging. Also, the sand is more compact after a nourishment project, which is difficult for the sea turtles to go through. The dredging also creates a higher plane of sand, which brings the young hatchlings closer to the lights near the beach. The lights end up confusing the babies, and many of them die. Overall, dredging has not stopped sea turtles from nesting, but it has lessened the number of turtles doing so each year.

8. The correct answer is I (ship or boat).

Type of passage: Literary text

Benchmark: LA.A.1.3.2.

The correct answer is I. In this poem the word "vessel" is strictly used to describe a boat or ship that the captain sailed. None of the other choices match this use.

9. The correct answer is B (The author wants him to be alive and to know that he has been victorious).

Type of passage: Literary text

Benchmark: LA.A.2.3.1

The correct answer is B. The author or narrator of the poem says, "for you the flag is flung—for you the bugle trills. . . ." Clearly, the author wishes the captain were still alive to hear the sounds of victory.

©Copyright 2006 by Barron's Educational Series, Inc.

10. The correct answer is F (to compare the death of the captain to that of a great leader).

Type of passage: Literary text

Benchmark: LA.A.2.2.2

The correct answer is F. The captain's victory and unfortunate death can be compared to the fate of great leaders such as Abraham Lincoln and Martin Luther King, Jr.

11. The correct answer is A (a father).

Type of passage: Literary text

Benchmark: LA.A.2.2.7

The correct answer is A. In line 14 of the poem, the captain is referred to as "dear father."

12. The correct answer is H (heroic, great leader).

Type of passage: Literary text

Benchmark: LA.E.1.3.2

The correct answer is H. The title of captain implies that he is a leader; he is referred to as "dear father." Also, there is great sadness because the captain has died, but the poem mentions that he is victorious. Only a great leader who is respected in this manner would be considered a great, heroic leader.

13. Use the short-response scoring rubric in Chapter 5 to score this response (2-point scoring rubric).

Type of passage: Informational text

Benchmark: LA.E.1.3.3

A top-score response would include each example of irony appearing in the poem, specifically how the sounds of victory cannot even be heard by the captain who has died. For example:

Although he fought for his victory, the captain does not get to enjoy the "spoils" of his success. He has died, but did not get to enjoy the people cheering him, the flags being flung in his honor, or the sound of the bells and the bugle. All of these sights and sounds are for the captain, yet he has died and cannot enjoy them.

14. The correct answer is C (evoke emotion in the reader).

Type of passage: Literary text

LA.A.2.3.2

The correct answer is C. The entire poem is filled with irony to make the reader feel sorry that the captain has died without being able to enjoy the spoils of his victory.

15. The correct answer is I (mournful).

Type of passage: Literary text

Benchmark: LA.E.1.3.4.

The correct answer is I. The image of a dead, honored captain is repeated over and over, and the reader is left feeling mournful because of the loss of such a great leader. Therefore, the mood of this poem is mournful.

16. Use the extended-response scoring rubric in Chapter 5 to score this response (4-point scoring rubric).

Type of passage: Informational text

Benchmark: LA.E.1.3.3

A top-score response would include specific examples of imagery including the sounds, sights, and feelings mentioned in the poem. Then a brief statement would be made about how these images contribute to the development of the poem. For example:

Imagery plays an important role in being able to experience a poem. The author used the images of blood to evoke emotion in the reader. Being able to picture a gruesome sight makes the reader feel sorry for the captain. The sounds of victory like the bugle and the bells can be imagined by the reader also. And finally, the picture of many people cheering on a captain for his victory, but he has died, is overwhelming. All of these images definitely lead the reader to have compassion and sympathy for the captain.

17. The correct answer is D (He relaxes).

Type of passage: Literary text

Benchmark: LA.E.1.3.2

The correct answer is D. Greg relaxes because he sees a homeless man who appears to be more scared than he is. He knows Lemon Brown won't try to hurt him and relaxes.

©Copyright 2006 by Barron's Educational Series, Inc.

18. Use the short-response scoring rubric in Chapter 5 to score this response (2-point scoring rubric).

Type of passage: Literary text

Benchmark: LA.E.1.3.3

A top-score response would include the rationale for why Lemon Brown says, "Every man got a treasure." For example:

Lemon Brown says, "Every man got a treasure" because he believes that treasure is not a physical or monetary reward. He believes that each man has something inside himself that is full of worth. He encourages Greg to think of what his treasure is. Lemon Brown does not believe that every man is rich or has buried treasure in his yard!

19. The correct answer is F (The blues gave up on him).

Type of passage: Literary text

Benchmark: LA.E.1.3.3

The correct answer is F. Lemon Brown says, "You don't give up the blues; they give you up."

20. The correct answer is D (Lemon Brown was a bit afraid).

Type of passage: Literary text

Benchmark: LA.E.1.3.3

The correct answer is D. Lemon Brown believes the men are going to steal his treasure because he hears the men say, "We heard you talking about your treasure. . . . We just want to see it, that's all." But Lemon Brown hears them pick up a pipe.

21. The correct answer is I (He thought they were going to steal it).

Type of Passage: Literary text

Benchmark: LA.E.1.3.3

The correct answer is I. When Lemon Brown first meets Greg, he says to him: "You ain't one of them bad boys looking for my treasure, is you? Because I told you I got me a razor." So when he and Greg hear the men downstairs, Lemon Brown says, "They's bad men." Even though the men call out that they just want to see the treasure, Lemon Brown believes they want to actually steal it.

22. The correct answer is B (rough and ragged).

Type of passage: Literary text

Benchmark: LA.A.1.3.2.

The correct answer is B. A gnarled hand is rough and ragged. It can be smaller than normal size but not necessarily. The only choice that can be true in all circumstances is B.

23. The correct answer is H (a homeless man).

Type of passage: Literary text

Benchmark: LA.E.1.3.2

The correct answer is H. Because he lives in an abandoned building, Lemon Brown is probably homeless. All the other choices would require more information to be given in the story.

24. Use the extended-response scoring rubric in Chapter 5 to score this response. (4-point scoring rubric).

Type of passage: Literary text

Benchmark: LA.E.1.3.3

A top-score response would state that the theme of the poem is that the real worth of a person is not in riches. For example:

The theme of "The Treasure of Lemon Brown" is that the real worth of man is not of monetary value, but in his self-confidence and self-worth. The author clearly wanted to portray Lemon Brown as a man with no money, nothing to his name, but the richness of his self-worth. The title is so appropriate in explaining the theme of this story because the "treasure of Lemon Brown" is that he has discovered his own worth, something that cannot be taken away from him, but also something that is only of value to him.

25. The correct answer is A (was an infant).

Type of passage: Literary text

Benchmark: LA.E.1.3.2

The correct answer is A. The first line of the story gives away this answer: "When Pecos Bill was a little baby. . . ."

©Copyright 2006 by Barron's Educational Series, Inc.

26. The correct answer is H (Before they turned each other into catfish bait, Bill fell out of the wagon and landed kerplop on the sun-scorched desert).

Type of passage: Literary text

Benchmark: LA.E.1.3.3

The correct answer is H. Onomatopoeia is the use of a word that is pronounced like the sound being described. Kerplop is the sound something makes when it falls; therefore, the only sentence that would match is the one containing the word "kerplop."

27. The correct answer is C ("Nice to meet you").

Type of passage: Literary text

Benchmark: LA.A.1.3.2.

The correct answer is C. In the story the author writes, "'Goo-goo' happens to mean something similar to 'Glad to meet you' in coyote language." The only choice that matches this is C.

28. The correct answer is H (moving out west).

Type of passage: Literary text

Benchmark: LA.E.1.3.2

The correct answer is H. The second paragraph gives the answer to this question: "Before sundown Bill's folks loaded their fifteen kids and all their belongings into their covered wagon and started west." The only choice that mentions heading west is H.

29. The correct answer is A (a pack of coyotes).

Type of passage: Literary text

Benchmark: LA.E.1.3.2

The correct answer is A. The story states, "Before he knew it, he was roaming the prairies with the pack." The story goes on to explain the activities Pecos Bill performed with the coyotes, implying that they raised him.

30. The correct answer is I (acted like a baby).

Type of Passage: Literary text

Benchmark: LA.A.2.3.1

The correct answer is I. The last paragraph describes Pecos Bill doing all of the other activities listed.

31. Use the short-response scoring rubric in Chapter 5 to score this response (2-point scoring rubric).

Type of passage: Literary text

Benchmark: LA.E.1.3.2

A top-score response would include the details of how Pecos Bill lost his family on their trip out west. For example:

Pecos Bill, his fourteen siblings and his parents were moving out west to get away from close neighbors. Along the way, Bill started picking fights with his brothers and sisters. Everyone started pushing and shoving, and eventually Bill fell out of the wagon. No one noticed that he had fallen out until it was too late to try to find him.

32. Use the short-response scoring rubric in Chapter 5 to score this response (2-point scoring rubric).

Type of passage: Literary text

Benchmark: LA.E.1.3.3

A top-score response would include examples of similes, alliteration, figurative language, and onomatopoeia. For example:

There are many literary devices used in this tall tale to help the reader picture what is going on in the story. First of all, there are similes that use "like" or "as." For example, Bill is described as "as tough as a pine knot." Another example is alliteration, where the same sound is repeated in one sentence: "Baby Bill." The repetition of the "b" sound mimics the sound a baby makes. Finally, figurative language such as onomatopoeia is used: "kerplop," "rattle," and "sniff."

33. The correct answer is C (early 1800s).

Type of passage: Informational text

Benchmark: LA.E.1.3.2

The correct answer is C. The article states that the Creek War took place in 1813–1814, which is the early 1800s.

©Copyright 2006 by Barron's Educational Series, Inc.

34. The correct answer is F (to escape the effects of the First Seminole War).

Type of passage: Informational text

Benchmark: LA.E.2.2.1

The correct answer is F. The article states, "After the first series of encounters, known as the First Seminole War (1814–1818), many Native families moved further into the peninsula." This implies that the "encounters" (the burning of Native villages and the killing of resistance leaders) after the war caused the Seminoles to move.

35. The correct answer is B (runaway slaves).

Type of passage: Informational text

Benchmark: LA.A.1.3.2.

The correct answer is B. The article mentions "Black Seminoles" who were "fierce fighters" who aided the Seminoles in their resistance.

36. Use the short-response scoring rubric in Chapter 5 to score this response (2-point scoring rubric).

Type of passage: Informational text

Benchmark: LA.A.1.3.2.

A top-score response would include the origin of the Seminole name. Specifically, information about the meaning of the term "free people" should be included in the answer. For example:

In Maskókî, there was a phrase "istî siminolî," which meant "free people." This term sounds very much like "seminole." The Seminoles were referred to as "free people" because they had not been ruled by the Spaniards or the English in their native land.

37. The correct answer is I (the Second Seminole War).

Type of passage: Informational text

Benchmark: LA.A.1.3.2.

The correct answer is I. The article states, "This one, the Second Seminole War (1835–42), would be the longest, most costly, and the last of the US's Wars of Indian Removal . . . ."

38. The correct answer is D (Tallahassee).

Type of passage: Informational text

LA.A.1.3.4.

The correct answer is D. The article says that the Seminole Tribe has five reservations across the peninsula of Florida in Hollywood, Big Cypress, Brighton, Immokalee, and Tampa. Tallahassee is not one of the cities mentioned.

39. The correct answer is I (all of the above).

Type of passage: Informational text

Benchmark: LA.A.1.3.2.

The correct answer is I. The article says that in the late 1800s, "white traders, Christian missionaries, and US government agents began to enter their territory once again." Therefore, the only answer choice is "all of the above."

40. The correct answer is B (Seminole Indians).

Type of passage: Informational text

Benchmark: LA.A.1.3.2.

The correct answer is B. The very first sentence mentions this answer, that Seminoles built towns and villages before the coming of Europeans to southeastern North America, implying that the Seminoles were the first to settle Florida.

41. The correct answer is H (thousands of kilometers per hour).

Type of passage: Informational text

Benchmark: LA.A.1.3.2.

The correct answer is H. The end of the third paragraph states, "These tracks would allow electromagnetic vehicles to travel at speeds reaching thousands of kilometers-per-hour."

©Copyright 2006 by Barron's Educational Series, Inc.

42. The correct answer is C (electromagnetic vehicle).

Type of passage: Informational text

Benchmark: LA.A.1.3.2.

The correct answer is C. The end of the third paragraph states, "These tracks would allow electromagnetic vehicles to travel at speeds reaching thousands of kilometers-per-hour."

43. The correct answer is H (late 1990).

Type of passage: Informational text

Benchmark: LA.A.1.3.2.

The correct answer is H. The article refers to the "1999 workshop" indicating that the workshop was held in the late 1990s.

44. The correct answer is A (cut costs for NASA).

Type of passage: Informational text

Benchmark: LA.A.2.3.1

The correct answer is A. The article refers to the space elevator as a "cost-cutting device for NASA."

45. Use the extended-response scoring rubric in Chapter 5 to score this response (4-point scoring rubric).

Type of passage: Informational text

LA.A.2.3.2

A top-score response would include an opinion as to whether or not a space elevator will be built with a list of at least two reasons. For example:

It is possible that a space elevator will be built in the future. Besides the fact that NASA has held workshops discussing the possibility of these "electromagnetic vehicles," it would be humanly possible to build the necessary tracks and platforms needed to run a space elevator. Although it seems pretty unrealistic, scientists are actually studying the exact materials needed for construction and the best locations for a space elevator. With new technology, it is very possible to even build a space elevator that can withstand hurricanes. The amount of research poured into this topic suggests that at some point NASA will be working on this cheaper mode of transportation to the moon!

FCAT WRITING+ TEST ANSWERS AND EXPLANATIONS

Note to students:
As you read through the correct answers, pay close attention to the explanations of the answers. The Florida Sunshine State Standards listed as benchmarks for each question tell you what type of skill is being tested in the question. (A complete list of the benchmarks can be found in the Appendix.)

Note to parents and teachers:
Pay close attention to the benchmarks listed. They indicate the type of skill being tested in each particular question, according to the Florida Sunshine State Standards. Use these skills to provide similar practice before the test. (A complete list of the benchmarks can be found in the Appendix.)

1. The correct answer is B (Important people).

Item type: Stimulus-based

Category: Focus

Benchmark: L.A.B.1.3.1.

The correct answer is B. Generals and commanders were important people in the Civil War. They would not logically fit under any other subtopic listed.

2. The correct answer is G (a paper that explains and summarizes the major points of the Civil War).

Item type: Stimulus-based

Category: Focus

Benchmark: L.A.B.1.3.1.

The correct answer is G. Major points of the Civil War are listed as subtopics.

©Copyright 2006 by Barron's Educational Series, Inc.

3. The correct answer is D (all of the above).

Item type: Stimulus-based

Category: Focus

Benchmark: L.A.B.1.3.1.

The correct answer is D. Thousands of deaths, a divided country, and divided families are all possible results of war. Therefore, "all of the above" is the only logical answer.

4. The correct answer is F (Beethoven, Bach, Chopin).

Item type: Stimulus-based

Category: Organization

Benchmark: L.A.B.1.3.1.

The correct answer is F. The third subtopic is "Classical music helps learning" because Beethoven, Bach, and Chopin are all classical music composers.

5. The correct answer is A (short for a research paper).

Item type: Stimulus-based

Category: Focus

Benchmark: L.A.B.1.3.1.

The correct answer is A. This topic would not be too short for a research paper. It would be too broad for an essay, too vague for a personal letter, and too detailed for an editorial.

6. The correct answer is F (Good effects).

Item type: Stimulus-based

Category: Organization

Benchmark: L.A.B.1.3.1.

The correct answer is F. Benefits imply good effects.

7. The correct answer is C (sentence 11).

Item type: Sample-based

Category: Conventions

Benchmark: LA.B.1.3.3.

The correct answer is C. "Then theirs the coughing from the burning sensation in your throat from second hand smoke." "Theirs" means "belongs to them"; the correct spelling is "there's" or "there is."

8. The correct answer is I (sentence 10).

Item type: Sample-based

Category: Support

Benchmark: LA.B.1.3.2.

The correct answer is I. Sentence 10 should be deleted because is mentions the inhaler and calling a doctor, which do not relate directly to the topic of secondhand smoke being dangerous.

9. The correct answer is D (sentence 19).

Item type: Sample-based

Category: Focus

Benchmark: LA.B.1.3.2.

The correct answer is D. The sentence "I know airports already have designated areas" is off topic for a conclusion about the dangers of secondhand smoke.

10. The correct answer is F (at the end of paragraph 1).

Item type: Sample-based

Category: Organization

Benchmark: LA.B.1.3.2.

The correct answer is F. The sentence is a persuasive argument that states the main

idea of the essay. If a similar sentence were not in the concluding paragraph, choice I would have been a better choice. However, because a similar statement is made in the conclusion, it is best placed in the introductory paragraph.

11. The correct answer is B (Let's do what we can to prevent the dangers of secondhand smoke).

Item type: Sample-based

Category: Focus

Benchmark: LA.B.2.3.2.

The correct answer is B. This choice is the only one with a call to action that restates the main opinion of the essay.

12. The correct answer is F (He wants to convince the reader to make a stand against secondhand smoke).

Item type: Sample-based

Category: Support

Benchmark: LA.B.2.3.2.

The correct answer is F. Darnel wants the reader to agree with him that secondhand smoke is bad by listing reasons why. Then he makes a call to the reader to make a stand against it.

©Copyright 2006 by Barron's Educational Series, Inc.

13. The correct answer is B (Jolly is my favorite pet).

Item type: Sample-based

Category: Support

Benchmark: L.A.B.2.3.3.

The correct answer is B. Mike writes simply and clearly. The only sentence that matches that same style (without a lot of wordy descriptions) is choice B.

14. The correct answer is H (One day she got out of her cage and caused a lot of problems in the house).

Item type: Sample-based

Category: Conventions

Benchmark: LA.B.1.3.3.

The correct answer is H. This is the only correct version of this sentence. The words "caused" and "a lot" are misspelled in the other choices.

15. The correct answer is A (sentence 7).

Item type: Sample-based

Category: Focus

Benchmark: LA.B.1.3.2.

The correct answer is A. Sentence 7 should be deleted because it mentions action unrelated to the rest of the paragraph, which talks about why Jolly is happy.

16. The correct answer is I (Another time when Jolly got out of her cage, she scared my mother in the kitchen).

Item type: Sample-based

Category: Support

Benchmark: LA.B.1.3.2.

The correct answer is I. Because the essay is about the "misadventures of Jolly" and only one adventure was listed, another paragraph about another adventure could logically follow Mike's third paragraph.

17. The correct answer is A (I also named her Jolly because of the way she spends her time).

Item type: Sample-based

Category: Focus

Benchmark: LA.B.1.3.2.

The correct answer is A. The second paragraph talks about how Jolly spends her time being happy or jolly; therefore a topic sentence stating this is appropriate.

18. The correct answer is G (Jolly was so scared; I've never seen her run so fast in my life).

Item type: Sample-based

Category: Conventions

Benchmark: LA.B.1.3.3.

The correct answer is G. This sentence is made up of two complete sentences. From the answer choices given, only the one with two clauses joined by a semicolon is correct.

19. The correct answer is C (last sentence of paragraph 2).

Item type: Sample-based

Category: Organization

Benchmark: LA.B.1.3.2.

The correct answer is C. The sentence "Another idea I had was to sell bracelets" does not support the paragraph because it brings up another idea apart from the babysitting idea.

20. The correct answer is I (I needed to come up with a name that was catchy, so I settled on Tyra's Tots).

Item type: Sample-based

Category: Conventions

Benchmark: LA.B.1.3.3.

The correct answer is I. Both words in the name of her business must be capitalized; it should not have quotation marks surrounding it, and it should not be underlined. Also, the apostrophe should be before the "s" in "Tyra's," showing possession.

21. The correct answer is B (Each of us has regular clients).

Item type: Sample-based

Category: Conventions

Benchmark: LA.B.1.3.3.

The correct answer is B. The singular subject "each" is a collective noun that must have a singular verb, "has."

22. The correct answer is I (Before I could be open for business,).

Item type: Sample-based

Category: Organization

Benchmark: LA.B.1.3.2.

The correct answer is I. "Before I could be open for business" transitions the reader from the idea for a business to the planning of the business.

©Copyright 2006 by Barron's Educational Series, Inc.

23. The correct answer is D (After creating a name and a slogan, I needed to get the word out!).

Item type: Sample-based

Category: Conventions

Benchmark: LA.B.1.3.2.

The correct answer is D. The introductory phrase, "After creating a name and a slogan" refers to what Tyra did. The following subject must be "Tyra"; because the essay is written in the first person, the subject must be "I."

24. The correct answer is G (The best part is that I'm very close to having enough money to buy that mountain bike).

Item type: Sample-based

Category: Focus

Benchmark: LA.B.1.3.2.

The correct answer is G. To tie in the reason why Tyra started her own business in the first place, to earn money to purchase a mountain bike, must be repeated in the conclusion. Remember, do not bring up any new information in a conclusion.

25. The correct answer is C (Tryouts for the eighth grade drama presentation, *The Diary of Anne Frank*, will be held next week after school in the theatre from Monday until Wednesday).

Item type: Sample-based

Category: Conventions

Benchmark: LA.B.1.3.3.

The correct answer is C. One word was misspelled in the original sentence: "eighth." "Theatre" should not be capitalized unless it is the first word in a sentence or part of the theatre's name. Choice D is the only choice that corrects both errors.

26. The correct answer is H (sentence 7).

Item type: Sample-based

Category: Support

Benchmark: LA.B.1.3.2.

The correct answer is H. Sentence 7 repeats the warning that incomplete packets will keep a student from auditioning.

27. The correct answer is A (In addition to cast members,).

Item type: Sample-based

Category: Organization

Benchmark: LA.B.1.3.2.

The correct answer is A. The paragraph talks about other jobs open besides cast members. The only logical transitional phrase is "In addition to cast members."

28. The correct answer is F (All students interested must pick up an application packet from one of the drama teachers by Friday afternoon and bring it completed to the audition, or they will not be eligible to audition).

Item type: Sample-based

Category: Support

Benchmark: LA.B.1.3.2.

The correct answer is F. This answer is the only one that indicates when the packet is due, Friday afternoon.

29. The correct answer is D (props).

Item type: Sample-based

Category: Support

Benchmark: LA.B.1.3.2.

The correct answer is D. Students are asked not to bring props to the audition.

30. The correct answer is H (sentence 14).

Item type: Sample-based

Category: Focus

Benchmark: LA.B.1.3.2.

The correct answer is H. Knowing that there are only five minor roles and that the rest are "pretty important" is not a necessary detail for students auditioning for the play.

31. The correct answer is B (plants).

Item type: Cloze-based

Category: Conventions

Benchmark: LA.B.1.3.3.

The correct answer is B. A herbivore eats plants; therefore "plants" should go in the blank.

©Copyright 2006 by Barron's Educational Series, Inc.

32. The correct answer is F (their).

Item type: Cloze-based

Category: Conventions

Benchmark: LA.B.1.3.3.

The correct answer is F. Sea grass beds are vital to the manatees' survival. In order to replace "manatees'," the word "their" must be used to show the plural possessive form.

33. The correct answer is A (sea cows).

Item type: Cloze-based

Category: Conventions

Benchmark: LA.B.1.3.3.

The correct answer is A. Another name for manatees is sea cows, but it is not a proper name and does not need to be capitalized.

34. The correct answer is H (move).

Item type: Cloze-based

Category: Conventions

Benchmark: LA.B.1.3.3.

The correct answer is H. The present tense is used throughout the article; therefore, the present tense "move" must be used in this sentence as well.

35. The correct answer is A (For example,).

Item type: Cloze-based

Category: Conventions

Benchmark: LA.B.1.3.3.

The correct answer is A. The first word in "For example," must be capitalized as it is the first word in the sentence. Also, a comma must be placed after "example" to set it off as an introductory phrase.

36. The correct answer is G (them).

Item type: Cloze-based

Category: Conventions

Benchmark: LA.B.1.3.3.

The correct answer is G. The article encourages students to look for manatees. To replace "manatees" with a pronoun, you must use the plural pronoun "them."

37. The correct answer is A (Florida's rivers and protected forests provide a natural habitat for many animals).

Item type: Stand-alone

Category: Conventions

Benchmark: LA.B.1.3.3.

The correct answer is A. The only words capitalized should be the first word in the sentence (also because it is a proper noun). The rest of the words should be lowercase.

38. The correct answer is H (Proud of her achievement, Jennie showed everyone her excellent report card).

Item type: Stand-alone

Category: Conventions

Benchmark: LA.B.1.3.3.

The correct answer is H. The introductory phrase, "Proud of her achievement," refers to Jennie; therefore the subject of the sentence should be "Jennie."

39. The correct answer is B (The teacher asked everyone to turn in his or her homework).

Item type: Stand-alone

Category: Conventions

Benchmark: LA.B.1.3.3.

The correct answer is B. The collective noun "everyone" must be replaced by a singular pronoun "his or her" or simply "his."

40. The correct answer is F (With a new head coach, the football team is expected to play well this year).

Item type: Stand-alone

Category: Conventions

Benchmark: LA.B.1.3.3.

The correct answer is F. There are two parts to look at in this sentence. First, the singular (collective) noun "team" must agree with the singular verb "is." Second, the adverb "well" must be used to describe how they will play.

©Copyright 2006 by Barron's Educational Series, Inc.

41. The correct answer is C (NASA plans to expand its research on several planets including Mars and Saturn).

Item type: Stand-alone

Category: Conventions

Benchmark: LA.B.1.3.3.

The correct answer is C. "NASA" is an abbreviation that uses all capital letters with no periods between the letters. Also, Mars and Saturn are proper nouns and should be capitalized.

42. The correct answer is G (The following items must be retrieved from the store: toothpaste, hand soap, shampoo, and conditioner).

Item type: Stand-alone

Category: Conventions

Benchmark: LA.B.1.3.3.

The correct answer is G. When writing a list, you should begin the list with a colon and place a comma after each item, even before the conjunction "and."

43. The correct answer is B (When writing an essay, it is important to write a clear topic sentence for each paragraph, which indicates the main idea to the reader).

Item type: Stand-alone

Category: Conventions

Benchmark: LA.B.1.3.3.

The correct answer is B. The word "which" is correct for this sentence. "Witch" is a noun, and "wich" is not a word.

44. The correct answer is F (The newspaper reporter was asked to write his news story thoroughly, accurately, and quickly).

Item type: Stand-alone

Category: Conventions

Benchmark: LA.B.1.3.3.

The correct answer is F. This sentence must have parallelism. Each adverb must be written in the same form, ending with "-ly."

45. The correct answer is C (Last year, my family moved to Central Florida).

Item type: Stand-alone

Category: Conventions

Benchmark: LA.B.1.3.3.

The correct answer is C. The correct tense for the sentence is the past tense because the action took place in the past. The first choice is not correct because it contains a singular subject "family" and a plural helping verb "have."

©Copyright 2006 by Barron's Educational Series, Inc.

FCAT PRACTICE TEST TWO ANSWER BOOKLET

Carefully remove this answer booklet and use it with Practice Test Two P2: FCAT Reading and Writing+ Tests.

FCAT Reading Test

Directions: Fill in the bubble for the answer you choose for each multiple-choice question. For your response to the READ/THINK/EXPLAIN questions, write your answer using complete sentences on the lines provided.

Beginning time: _____

1. Ⓐ Ⓑ Ⓒ Ⓓ   **2.** Ⓕ Ⓖ Ⓗ Ⓘ   **3.** Ⓐ Ⓑ Ⓒ Ⓓ

4. Ⓕ Ⓖ Ⓗ Ⓘ

5. READ/THINK/EXPLAIN answer (short response):

_____

_____

_____

_____

_____

6. Ⓐ Ⓑ Ⓒ Ⓓ

7. READ/THINK/EXPLAIN answer (extended response):

_____

_____

_____

_____

_____

_____

_____

_____

8. Ⓕ Ⓖ Ⓗ Ⓘ   **9.** Ⓐ Ⓑ Ⓒ Ⓓ   **10.** Ⓕ Ⓖ Ⓗ Ⓘ

11. Ⓐ Ⓑ Ⓒ Ⓓ   **12.** Ⓕ Ⓖ Ⓗ Ⓘ

13. READ/THINK/EXPLAIN answer (short response):

_____

_____

_____

_____

_____

14. Ⓐ Ⓑ Ⓒ Ⓓ   **15.** Ⓕ Ⓖ Ⓗ Ⓘ

16. READ/THINK/EXPLAIN answer (extended response):

_____

_____

_____

_____

_____

_____

_____

_____

_____

17. Ⓐ Ⓑ Ⓒ Ⓓ

18. READ/THINK/EXPLAIN answer (short response):

_____

_____

_____

_____

19. Ⓕ Ⓖ Ⓗ Ⓘ   **20.** Ⓐ Ⓑ Ⓒ Ⓓ   **21.** Ⓕ Ⓖ Ⓗ Ⓘ
22. Ⓐ Ⓑ Ⓒ Ⓓ   **23.** Ⓕ Ⓖ Ⓗ Ⓘ

©Copyright 2006 by Barron's Educational Series, Inc.

24. READ/THINK/EXPLAIN answer (extended response):

_____

_____

_____

_____

_____

_____

_____

_____

_____

25. Ⓐ Ⓑ Ⓒ Ⓓ   **26.** Ⓕ Ⓖ Ⓗ Ⓘ   **27.** Ⓐ Ⓑ Ⓒ Ⓓ

28. Ⓕ Ⓖ Ⓗ Ⓘ   **29.** Ⓐ Ⓑ Ⓒ Ⓓ   **30.** Ⓕ Ⓖ Ⓗ Ⓘ

31. READ/THINK/EXPLAIN answer (short response):

_____

_____

_____

_____

32. READ/THINK/EXPLAIN answer (short response):

_____

_____

_____

_____

_____

33. Ⓐ Ⓑ Ⓒ Ⓓ   **34.** Ⓕ Ⓖ Ⓗ Ⓘ   **35.** Ⓐ Ⓑ Ⓒ Ⓓ

36. READ/THINK/EXPLAIN answer (short response):

_____

_____

_____

_____

_____

37. Ⓕ Ⓖ Ⓗ Ⓘ   **38.** Ⓐ Ⓑ Ⓒ Ⓓ   **39.** Ⓕ Ⓖ Ⓗ Ⓘ

40. Ⓐ Ⓑ Ⓒ Ⓓ   **41.** Ⓕ Ⓖ Ⓗ Ⓘ   **42.** Ⓐ Ⓑ Ⓒ Ⓓ

43. Ⓕ Ⓖ Ⓗ Ⓘ   **44.** Ⓐ Ⓑ Ⓒ Ⓓ

©Copyright 2006 by Barron's Educational Series, Inc.

45. READ/THINK/EXPLAIN answer (extended response):

_____

_____

_____

_____

_____

_____

_____

_____

Ending time: _____

FCAT Writing+ Test (Essay)

Beginning time: _____

Planning Sheet

©Copyright 2006 by Barron's Educational Series, Inc.

Essay Sheet

_____

_____

_____

_____

_____

_____

_____

_____

_____

_____

_____

_____

_____

_____

_____

_____

_____

_____

_____

_____

_____

_____

Ending time: _____

©Copyright 2006 by Barron's Educational Series, Inc.

FCAT Wrting+ Test (Multiple-Choice)

Directions: Fill in the bubble for the answer you choose for each multiple-choice question.

Beginning time: _____

1. Ⓐ Ⓑ Ⓒ Ⓓ

2. Ⓕ Ⓖ Ⓗ Ⓘ

3. Ⓐ Ⓑ Ⓒ Ⓓ

4. Ⓕ Ⓖ Ⓗ Ⓘ

5. Ⓐ Ⓑ Ⓒ Ⓓ

6. Ⓕ Ⓖ Ⓗ Ⓘ

7. Ⓐ Ⓑ Ⓒ Ⓓ

8. Ⓕ Ⓖ Ⓗ Ⓘ

9. Ⓐ Ⓑ Ⓒ Ⓓ

10. Ⓕ Ⓖ Ⓗ Ⓘ

11. Ⓐ Ⓑ Ⓒ Ⓓ

12. Ⓕ Ⓖ Ⓗ Ⓘ

13. Ⓐ Ⓑ Ⓒ Ⓓ

14. Ⓕ Ⓖ Ⓗ Ⓘ

15. Ⓐ Ⓑ Ⓒ Ⓓ

16. Ⓕ Ⓖ Ⓗ Ⓘ

17. Ⓐ Ⓑ Ⓒ Ⓓ

18. Ⓕ Ⓖ Ⓗ Ⓘ

19. Ⓐ Ⓑ Ⓒ Ⓓ

20. Ⓕ Ⓖ Ⓗ Ⓘ

21. Ⓐ Ⓑ Ⓒ Ⓓ

22. Ⓕ Ⓖ Ⓗ Ⓘ

23. Ⓐ Ⓑ Ⓒ Ⓓ

24. Ⓕ Ⓖ Ⓗ Ⓘ

25. Ⓐ Ⓑ Ⓒ Ⓓ

26. Ⓕ Ⓖ Ⓗ Ⓘ

27. Ⓐ Ⓑ Ⓒ Ⓓ

28. Ⓕ Ⓖ Ⓗ Ⓘ

29. Ⓐ Ⓑ Ⓒ Ⓓ

30. Ⓕ Ⓖ Ⓗ Ⓘ

31. Ⓐ Ⓑ Ⓒ

32. Ⓕ Ⓖ Ⓗ

33. Ⓐ Ⓑ Ⓒ

34. Ⓕ Ⓖ Ⓗ

35. Ⓐ Ⓑ Ⓒ

36. Ⓕ Ⓖ Ⓗ

37. Ⓐ Ⓑ Ⓒ

38. Ⓕ Ⓖ Ⓗ

39. Ⓐ Ⓑ Ⓒ

40. Ⓕ Ⓖ Ⓗ

41. Ⓐ Ⓑ Ⓒ

42. Ⓕ Ⓖ Ⓗ

43. Ⓐ Ⓑ Ⓒ

44. Ⓕ Ⓖ Ⓗ

45. Ⓐ Ⓑ Ⓒ

Ending time: _____

©Copyright 2006 by Barron's Educational Series, Inc.

PREPARING FOR THE FCATs?
Barron's Has the Answers!

Teachers and their students preparing for Florida's statewide eighth grade level and tenth grade level exams will find plenty of help from Barron's. All titles present extensive subject reviews, practice tests with answers, study advice, and test-taking tips.

For Eighth Graders—

Barron's Grade 8 FCAT in Reading and Writing +
Kelly Battles
This classroom aid prepares eighth graders with subject reviews in English grammar, sentence construction, the fundamentals of essay writing, and reading comprehension. All review sections are supplemented with practice questions and answers. Two full-length practice FCAT tests in Reading and Writing are presented with answers.
Paperback, 288 pp., ISBN-10: 0-7641-3316-0, ISBN-13: 978-0-7641-3316-9, $11.99, Canada $16.99

Let's Prepare for the FCAT Grade 8 Math Exam
Pamela Windspirit, M.Ed.
Florida's eighth-grade students will be ready for the exam with this manual. It provides two full-length sample tests with explained answers plus a 20-lesson subject review covering all topics. They include whole numbers and decimals; operations on numbers; fractions; rates, ratios, proportions, and scale drawings; percents; geometry basics; angles; polygons; powers and roots; the Pythagorean theorem, and much more.
Paperback, 272 pp., ISBN-10: 0-7641-3193-1, ISBN-13: 978-0-7641-3193-6, $11.99, Canada $17.50

For Tenth Graders—

How to Prepare for the Grade 10 Florida Comprehensive Assessment Tests in Reading and Writing
Claudine Townley
This manual prepares Florida tenth-grade students with test-taking advice and an explanation of how the test is scored. Subject review focuses on practice exercises in vocabulary, the several aspects of reading comprehension, and knowledge of literary elements. Two complete practice tests are presented with answers to all questions. A five-chapter unit instructs on the elements of essay writing and presents sample essays.
Paperback, 270 pp., ISBN-10: 0-7641-2746-2, ISBN-13: 978-0-7641-2746-5, $14.95, Canada $21.95

How to Prepare for the High School Math Florida Comprehensive Assessment Test
Pamela Windspirit, M.A.
Tenth grade students in Florida will find extensive math preparation with a diagnostic test and two full-length practice tests. All questions come with answer keys and explanations. Review chapters cover number sense, concepts, and operations; measurement; geometry and spatial sense; algebraic thinking; and data analysis and probability. A general introduction to the FCAT explains the test format and helps students identify their strengths and weaknesses.
Paperback, 332 pp., ISBN-10: 0-7641-2158-8, ISBN-13: 978-0-7641-2158-6, $14.95, Canada $21.0

Barron's Educational Series, Inc.
250 Wireless Boulevard
Hauppauge, New York 11788

In Canada: Georgetown Book Warehouse
34 Armstrong Avenue
Georgetown, Ontario L7G 4R9

Visit our web site at:
www.barronseduc.com

Books may be purchased at your bookstore, or by mail from Barron's. Enclose check or money order for total amount plus sales tax where applicable and 18% for postage (minimum charge $5.95). New York, New Jersey, Michigan, Tennessee, and California residents add sales tax. All books are paperback editions. Prices subject to change without notice.

(#144) R 7/06